S0-ARL-005

DARWIN

Also by Ruth Padel

POETRY

Alibi

Summer Snow

Angel

Fusewire

Rembrandt Would Have Loved You

Voodoo Shop

The Soho Leopard

CRITICISM

52 Ways of Looking at a Poem

Alfred Lord Tennyson: Poems with Introduction and Notes

The Poem and the Journey

NONFICTION

In and Out of the Mind: Greek Images of the Tragic Self

Whom Gods Destroy: Elements of Greek and Tragic Madness

I'm a Man: Sex, Gods, and Rock 'n' Roll

Tigers in Red Weather

DARWIN

A LIFE IN POEMS

Ruth Padel

ALFRED A. KNOPF
NEW YORK
2009

THIS IS A BORZOI BOOK
PUBLISHED BY ALFRED A. KNOPF

www.aaknopf.com

Knopf, Borzoi Books, and the colophon are registered trademarks of Random House, Inc.

Originally published in Great Britain by Chatto & Windus, Random House Group Ltd., London.

Grateful acknowledgement is made to The Gwen Raverat Estate for permission to reprint an excerpt from *Period Piece* by Gwen Raverat (London: Faber and Faber Ltd., 1952). Reprinted by permission of The Gwen Raverat Estate.

Library of Congress Cataloguing-in-Publication Data

Padel, Ruth, [date]
Darwin : a life in poems / by Ruth Padel.—1st American ed.
p. cm.
ISBN 978-0-307-27239-3
1. Darwin, Charles, 1809–1882—Poetry. I. Title.
PR6066.A2739D37 2009
821'.914—dc22
2008053493

Manufactured in the United States of America
First United States Edition

For Oliver, Nicola, Felix and Adam
with much love

I believe you will humanize me.

Charles Darwin, Letter to Emma Wedgwood, 1838

CONTENTS

CHAPTER ONE
Boy (1809–1831)

CHAPTER TWO
Journey (1831–1836)

CHAPTER THREE
City (1837–1838)

CHAPTER FOUR
Emma (1838–1851)

CHAPTER FIVE

The Coat of Fur (1851–1882)

AUTHOR'S NOTE AND ACKNOWLEDGEMENTS

Thanks to the editors at the *London Review of Books*, *Poetry Review* and *The Wolf*, where some of these poems first appeared. Twenty poems were originally commissioned by the Bristol Festival of Ideas, www.ideasfestival.co.uk, to celebrate the bicentenary of Charles Darwin in 2009. They first appeared in Ruth Padel, *A Voyage Round Charles Darwin* (published by BCDP: Bristol, December 2008). They included, or were amalgamated into, 'Finding the Name in the Flower'; 'He Discovers a New Source of Joy'; 'The Problem of Pain'; 'Bliss Castle'; 'A Desperate Way to Avoid Paying Your Tailor'; 'Cat o' Nine Tails'; 'On Not Thinking About Variation in Tortoise-Shell'; 'He Finds His Own Definition of Grandeur'; 'On the Propagation of Mistletoe'; 'She Thinks the Hairs Under His Arm Grow Like a Crescent Moon'; 'The Confession'; 'The Pond Spirit'; 'The Devil's Chaplain'; 'A Crunch on the Gravel'; 'Your Words Have Come True with a Vengeance'; 'The Open Window' and 'I Made His Coffin Just the Way He Wanted It, All Rough'.

Some poems were also commissioned by the Contemporary Arts Programme at the Natural History Museum, London, for the exhibition *After Darwin: Contemporary Expressions*, 26 June to 29 November 2009. These included, or were amalgamated into, 'The Year My Mother Died'; 'The Miser'; 'Barmouth'; 'Wonders of the World'; 'He Discovers a New Source of Joy' and 'Notebook M'.

I am very grateful for these commissions, particularly because of a conversation I remember with my grandmother, Nora Barlow. Nora was Charles Darwin's granddaughter and edited several of his books, including the first unexpurgated version of his *Autobiography*, written in 1876 and originally published after he died by his son Francis, who, at his mother's request, removed a key passage about Charles's attitude to Christianity. When Nora edited the book she put this passage back. Many years afterwards, when she was ninety-five and I was looking after her one rainy summer in Cambridge, she talked to me about Charles's ideas and his sense of how they affected the faith of his wife, Emma.

Charles wrote his *Autobiography* in old age for his family. Emma, though she knew his developing views on religion from the first conversation they had after they were engaged (see p. 67, 'He Ignores His Father's Advice'), remained a devout and practising Christian. She and their children were his intended readers for the *Autobiography*. But when describing in it how he turned away from Christianity, he says he felt evidence was needed, 'to make any sane man believe in the miracles by which Christianity is supported'. He was always anxious to be honest. The more we know, he said, 'of the fixed laws of nature, the more incredible do miracles become'. He also said he was reluctant at first to give up his own belief.

Evidence was what he cared about. He had had a classical education, so the evidence he dreamed of was new manuscripts being found which confirmed the Gospels. His degree was in Divinity; he knew the Gospels in Greek as well as English: he even took the Greek New Testament with him on the *Beagle*. (Though, as my sceptical granny points out in her Introduction to *The Voyage of the Beagle*, we don't know if he ever opened it.) But increasingly he felt such proof would be unlikely. So he came gradually 'to disbelieve in Christianity as a divine revelation'. This disbelief 'crept over me at a very slow rate, but was at last complete. The rate was so slow that I felt no distress'.

At this point come the words which Francis dropped: 'and have never since doubted even for a single second that my conclusion was correct. I can indeed hardly see how anyone ought to wish Christianity to be true; for if so the plain language of the text seems to show that the men who do not believe, and this would include my Father, Brother and almost all my best friends, will be everlastingly punished.' He adds beneath, in a new emphatic paragraph all on its own, 'And this is a damnable doctrine.'

Six months after he died, Emma bracketed all these words in the manuscript and wrote beside them, 'I should dislike the passage in brackets to be published. It seems to me raw. Nothing can be said too severe upon the doctrine of everlasting punishment for disbelief – but very few now wd. call that "Christianity" (tho' the words are there). There is the question of verbal inspiration comes in too. E. D. Oct. 1882.'

This was the problem passage which my grandmother, in 1956, put back in her edition. After it, Charles goes on to discuss what he calls 'The old argument from design in Nature, as given by Paley' (see below, 'The Coddington Microscope', Poems i and ii, pp. 17–19).

As a young man at Cambridge, and when he began his voyage on the *Beagle*, Charles whole-heartedly believed William Paley's argument. It was then called 'natural theology'. The essence of it is that design implies a designer: this is what has been revived as 'intelligent design'. But, Darwin says in the *Autobiography*, now 'the law of natural selection has been discovered', this argument has lost its power. 'We can no longer argue that the beautiful hinge of a bivalve shell must have been made by an intelligent being, like the hinge of a door by man. There seems to be no more design in the variability of organic beings, and in the action of natural selection, than in the course which the wind blows.'

He adds that he has discussed this subject 'at the end of my book' (meaning *The Variation of Animals and Plants Under Domestication*), 'and the argument there given has never, as far as I can see, been answered'.

Then he goes on to the problem of pain. The more I studied his Notebooks, the more I felt that pain was the factor that particularly swayed him against the idea of a benevolent Creator. 'Disease and pain in the world,' he wrote in 1838, 'and they talk of perfection?' Some writers, he says in 1876, 'are so much impressed with the amount of suffering in the world that they doubt whether there is more of misery or of happiness; whether the world is a good or bad one'. But, 'The world seems to have a generally beneficent arrangement . . . According to my judgment happiness decidedly prevails, though this would be very difficult to prove.' If it *were* proved, it would fit 'the effects we might expect from Natural Selection'. For if all members of a species 'habitually suffered to an extreme degree, they would neglect to propagate their kind'. He is not talking only about human beings. 'All sentient beings,' he says, seem to 'have been formed so as to enjoy, as a general rule, happiness'.

After his voyage on the *Beagle*, Charles was constantly sick. We shall never know why. Some people think it was all hypochondria, others that it was a disease he contracted in South America. There are many theories in between. Whatever it was, he suffered greatly from it; he also lost three adored children and watched them die in unalleviated suffering. And yet, while writing the *Autobiography*, he says he feels that happiness is the 'general rule'. Did he say so to please Emma? We shall never know. Despite their divergent views on religion, their relationship was a very intense partnership and a deep sustaining intimacy. What my grandmother said to me in Cambridge made me long to write about Charles and Emma. I did not know I would ever find a way of doing it – but these two commissions pushed me into trying. So many thanks to Andrew Kelly of the Bristol Festival of Ideas and Bergit Arends at the Natural History Museum.

Apart from the original commissions, I am very grateful to people who contributed to this book in other ways. First to my mother Hilda, Nora's daughter: not least for taking us to Galapagos, where she was forced to wonder from a boat deck exactly which of her swimsuited children and grandchildren sitting in a little dinghy would be eaten first by the young killer whales who kept diving beneath and jolting us upwards. (Just playing, I am sure.)

Thanks also to many scientists and conservationists who took me into tiger forest in Russia and China, and tropical and subtropical forest both in Brazil and more extensively in India, Nepal, Bhutan, Laos and Sumatra. It was a privilege to accompany and learn from them.

Heartfelt thanks also to Elaine Feinstein for her warm and perceptive comments and to Aamer Hussein for subtle commenting in early stages; to Pedro Ferreira, Kerin Hope, Nicholas de Lange and my sister Nicola Hall for responding to specific sections; to Daljit Nagra for commenting on the whole thing in detail while teaching an Arvon course; to Rabih Alameddine for advice on how separate parts become a whole and listening to a whole penultimate draft; and to Gwen Burnyeat, Fiona Sampson and Randal

Keynes for taking time out from pressing work of their own to comment on a first draft. All these comments and suggestions were immensely helpful. Finally, many many thanks to David Harsent for detailed out-of-house editorial comment on the final text; and to Clara Farmer, my editor at Chatto, for patient, warm support and editing.

Warmest thanks also to my cousin Randal for taking me to Down House and Downe village in Kent, where Charles and Emma settled in 1842. (The varied spellings are not a mistake: the village has been spelt Downe from the 1850s but the Darwins' home was always Down House.)

Randal's understanding – communicated in conversation, in email and in his book *Annie's Box* – of the growth of Darwin's thought and feeling, of Down and all its inhabitants, and of the relationship between Charles and Emma, has been a great and abiding inspiration. While at Down with Randal, I also realized, or I thought I did, something new about a different house and garden which my sister and brothers and I loved very dearly as children: Boswells, the home created and run by our grandmother Nora. It must, I suddenly thought, have caught from afar something of the atmosphere at Down.

Thanks also to several important books: Nora Barlow's Introductions to *Charles Darwin and the Voyage of the Beagle* (Pilot Press Ltd, 1945), *The Autobiography of Charles Darwin* (Collins, 1958) and *Darwin and Henslow, Letters 1831–1860* (John Murray, 1967); Gillian Beer's Introduction to *On the Origin of Species* (Penguin, 1996); Andrew Berry (ed.), *Infinite Tropics: An Alfred Russel Wallace Anthology* (Verso, 2002); John Bowlby, *Charles Darwin* (Hutchinson, 1990); Janet Browne, *Voyaging* and *The Power of Place* (Jonathan Cape, 1995 and 2002); Paul Ekman's Introduction to Charles Darwin, *The Expression of the Emotions in Man and Other Animals* (HarperCollins, 1998); Randal Keynes, *Annie's Box* (Fourth Estate, 2001); Richard Keynes, *Fossils, Finches and Fuegians* (HarperCollins, 2002); and Edna Healey, *Emma Darwin* (Headline, 2001).

Lastly, many thanks to Somerset House Trust for inviting me to be their first Writer in Residence and providing me with a lovely room on the river where many of the poems exploring Darwin's own time spent in London, as Secretary to the Geological Society in Somerset House, were written.

Quotations from Darwin in the poems are drawn from many sources—from his books, scientific papers, autobiography, journals, notebooks, drafts and letters. I reference them in the margin when it might be useful. I hope it is clear when they come from someone else, such as his colleague Alfred Russel Wallace or Emma in her journal and letters. The letter by Elizabeth Bishop, from which a line is quoted as the epigraph to Chapter Two, appears in full in *Elizabeth Bishop and Her Art*, edited by Lloyd Schwartz and Sybil Estess (University of Michigan Press, 1983); the extract from Gwen Raverat's *Period Piece*, which appears as the epigraph to 'A Sacred Feeling about Orchids', is reprinted by kind permission of Faber and Faber.

The external events of Darwin's life are voluminously recorded in his own writings (available on www.darwin-online.org.uk), other people's memoirs and a quite astonishing body of letters now available online in the wonderful Correspondence Project, www.darwinproject.ac.uk.

I have drawn from his *Autobiography* for events in early childhood (and also, for the first poem, from the memoir of a school-fellow). Many feelings, however, which the poems attribute to him, or imply, are of course interpretation.

As for the words: I have had to tinker with some of them as they became poems. But I have not changed their sense. Nor, I hope, what I most wanted to give: his voice.

Ruth Padel

London, November 2008

CHAPTER ONE

BOY

1809–1831

FINDING THE NAME IN THE FLOWER

I

THE CHAPEL SCHOOL

'He brought a flower to school. He said his mother
  taught him to look inside the blossom
and discover the name of the plant.
  I inquired how it could be done
but the lesson was not transmissible.'

A walk through the zebra maze, to the Unitarian
  chapel on Claremont Hill. What do they say,
the black stripes on white house-walls? He's afraid
  of the dogs on Baker Street. When boys play
he chews the inside of his mouth. He can never fight.

Darwin grew up in Shrewsbury, a medieval English town on the border of Wales, where his father built a house in 1800. Early in 1817, when he was a timid boy of seven, his mother enrolled him in a small school attached to the Chapel in town.

The words quoted here come from the earliest memory of Darwin by anyone other than his family: William Leighton, an older pupil at the school who later became a botanist.

II

THE YEAR MY MOTHER DIED

'I remember her sewing-table, curiously constructed.
  Her black velvet gown. Nothing else
except her death-bed. And my Father, crying.' No embrace.
  'My older sisters, in their great grief,
did not speak her name.' Her memory was silence.
  No memento of her face.

Darwin's mother Susanna, daughter of the potter Josiah Wedgwood, died young in July 1817, when Darwin was eight.

III

STEALING THE AFFECTION OF DOGS

He does not seem to have known half how much our father loved him.
Caroline Wedgwood, née Darwin

The Mount, Shrewsbury, 1817–20.

Bits of the world blow towards him and come apart
on the wind. He invents. He lies.
'I had a passion for dogs. They seemed to know.
I was adept in robbing their masters of their love.'
He steals apples from the orchard, gives them to boys
in a cottage and tells them to watch how fast he runs.
He climbs a beech by the wall of the locked kitchen garden
and dreams himself into the inner gloss
of raspberry canes. A forest, glowing in its net.
Emerald coal in a watchman's brazier.
He straddles the coping, fits a stick in the hole at the foot
of a flower-pot, and pulls. Peaches and plums
fall in. Enough to have begun an orchard of his own.
My father's. Valuable. The words hang in the trees
when the soft blobs are gone. He hides his loot
in shrubbery and runs to tell:
he has found a hoard of stolen fruit!

IV

THE MISER

The passion for collecting, which leads a man to be a miser, a virtuoso, or a systematic naturalist, was very strong in me. It was clearly innate. None of my sisters or brother had this taste.

Darwin, *Autobiography*

Cross the Welsh Bridge out of town, go up the hill
 on Frankwell Street and you'll see, above the Severn,
 brick pillars with the sandy bloom of an ageing dog.
Around the back, Father's surgery and waiting-room.

Darwin's father was an affluent doctor. The estate of his house, The Mount, bordered the River Severn.

Outside, the Stable Yard: hay chutes, a piggery and toolshed.
 Lower down, a bothy on the river bank
 where plates of jagged ice, harvested in winter from the river,
lean one against the other. A dairy, where these blocks are dragged

to cool the milk and cream. The Quarry Pool
 where he fishes for newts and tadpoles.
 Collecting: to assert control
over what's unbearable. To gather and to list.

'Stones, coins, franks, insects, minerals and shells.'
 Collect yourself: to smother what you feel,
 recall to order, summon in one place;
making, like Orpheus, a system against loss.

Darwin, *Autobiography*.

V

HE DOUBTS HUMANITY IS AN INNATE QUALITY

The Mount,
Shrewsbury, 1818.

'I can say in my own favour I was as a boy humane,
but I owed this entirely to my sisters' example
and instruction. I was fond of collecting wild birds' eggs

but never took more than one from a nest –
except once when, out of a sort of bravado, I took all.
I had a strong taste for angling. I would sit

any number of hours on the bank of a pond
watching the float. When I learned
I could kill the worms first with salt,

I never spitted a living worm. But one day,
as a very little boy, I acted cruelly: *I beat a puppy.*
I believe just to enjoy the sense of power.

The beating could not have been severe
for the puppy did not howl. I remember
the exact spot where the crime was committed.

This act lay heavier on my conscience
from my love of dogs being then, and for a long
time afterwards, a passion.'

VI

BARMOUTH

A child on a beach, alone.
  Grey-eyed, thickset, kneeling to look.
'A blowy day. A large black and scarlet
  hemipterous insect. Many moths

including *zygaena*. A *cicindela* –
  largest genus of the Tiger beetle –
not found in Shropshire.'

Why does every gentleman not
  become an ornithologist?
Gulls and cormorants take their way home
  at evening on a wild, irregular course.

In 1819, when Darwin was ten, his family went on holiday to Plas Edwards, or Barmouth, in North Wales.

VII

WONDERS OF THE WORLD

Between 1818 and 1825 Darwin went to Shrewsbury School, up the road from home, as a day boy. The curriculum was 'strictly classical': Latin and Greek which he did not enjoy.

His brother Erasmus, whom he idolized, was five years older.

'The clear geometrical proofs of Euclid.
The principle of the vernier of a barometer.
Sitting in the Old Library window, for hours,
reading Shakespeare's historical plays.
Disputing, with friends, the statements
in *Wonders of the World*.' Can one really use squid
ink to write? At home, he works in the toolshed
with his brother, on chemical experiments.

'They nicknamed me "Gas".
The headmaster publicly rebuked me
for wasting my time on useless subjects.
He called me a *poco curante*.
I did not know what it meant.
It seemed to me a fearful reproach.'

VIII

THE EFFICACY OF PRAYER

'I often had to run through town between the School
and home.' Slipping the shuts between one dark street
and the next: *Shoplatch, Mardol, Grope Lane,*
Butcher Row. 'Being very fleet
I was generally in time. But I often prayed
earnestly to God for aid.' *Gullet Passage, Bear Steps,*
Portobello, Murivance. 'I attributed my success
to prayer, marvelling how greatly I was helped.'

The medieval names for Shrewsbury's narrow streets and 'shuts' – the slip-passages between old buildings – are still in use.

IX

TREASURE MAP

The vivid delight in scenery then awakened in my mind has lasted longer than any other aesthetic pleasure.

Darwin, *Autobiography*

The world poured back and forth a daft number of times
between mountains and the drill-holes of his eyes.

Fissure and sky. Bronze grass, brown-glow bog
asphodel and purple heather. 'The Welsh Borders
with my elder brother!' Hours in a wet saddle.

In 1820 Erasmus took Charles for a riding tour in Pistyll Rhayader, North Wales.

His pony's stringy mane. Long wriggles of shadow
through drystone walls. A treasure map, painted by gods.

X

UGLY

Shrewsbury, 1824.

The streets take little nicks out of him.
Caroline says he's ugly. His feet smell.
Everyone's do, but his are worse –

so large and full of bunions. And his big nose!
He dwells in the congealing shell
of a giant tortoise. He's fifteen.

He slinks down back alleys of Shrewsbury,
not to be seen. As through the ravines
of Hades.

XI

HE DISCOVERS A NEW SOURCE OF JOY

The handle, red brown swirls in the grain. Shrewsbury, 1825.
The trigger, circled

with a metal oval like an egg.
Cocking it, the up-and-down

gracile, a swan's neck,
silver crest hugging the finger.

Smell of oil and black powder.
The sights. The secrecy and shine.

'On killing my first snipe
my excitement was so great

that from the trembling of my hands
I had much difficulty reloading my gun.'

THE PROBLEM OF PAIN

I

HE LOOKS FOR LODGINGS WITH HIS OLDER BROTHER

In 1825 Darwin's father Robert removed Charles from school, where he was not doing well, and sent him with Erasmus to read medicine at Edinburgh University, where Robert had himself studied medicine; as had *his* father, the poet and doctor Erasmus Darwin, before him.

High cliffs with copper shadows. Arthur's Seat.
    Two brothers in the world. He's sixteen
and bouncing on hot springs

of excitement. 'Bridge Street
    is the most extraordinary thing
I ever saw. We looked over the side

and saw beneath a stream
    of people instead of a river!
Light bedrooms are scarce articles

in Edinburgh. Most are little holes
    with neither light nor air.
Our lodgings,

Eleven Lothian Street,
    are very moderate. One pound six
shillings for two bedrooms and a sitting-room.'

A medical career! He enrols in physics,
    surgery, anatomy.
Materia Medica.

II

HAUNTED

He tried *numb*. He was good at that once. But the assault
    of the operating theatre was off the Richter scale
of self-deception. The amputation table: a drawn-out sobbing
    yell. The smells – bowels opening, sawn bone.
'Long before the blessed days of chloroform.'
    Next time it was a boy, screaming. Blood fell
from an opened brain. 'I rushed away before the operation
    was completed, nor did I ever attend again.'
Pity – all those boring Greek lessons – and Fear
    pounding up from earth's tragic core
with no skin in between. Outside, in iron rain
    and the scent of dogshit, he leaned against bricks
of the hospital and stared at a torn-up world.
    At the phantasmagoria of *unbearable*.
'The cases fairly haunted me for many a long year.'

III

HE HANGS OUT WITH A TAXIDERMIST

Edmonstone had been a slave on a Guiana plantation run by the ornithologist-traveller Charles Waterton (1782–1865), who took him on collecting expeditions and wrote these up in his *Waterton's Wanderings in South America*. Waterton taught him taxidermy, took him to Glasgow and freed him. At Edinburgh, Edmonstone stuffed birds for Professor Jameson's museum. Darwin paid him a guinea an hour for lessons in taxidermy. It was there he must have heard direct accounts of tropical forest for the first time.

John Edmonstone, the first black gentleman
he's ever seen; and in the same street,
number thirty-seven. 'I used to sit with him

often, for he was a very pleasant intelligent man.'
Sublimate of mercury, brittle feathers, avian
anatomy. The scalpel tease-and-settling of wings.

As he leaves for number eleven
he sees a harvest moon. A shadow-bruised melon
as over the Amazon.

IV

ON THE OVA OF *FLUSTRA*

Low tide on the Firth of Forth. Silvery
    and nothing to do with pain. Dark pines
on a headland; streaks of slime
    over charcoal rock with a vein of cream;

a bridge, an eyebrow against white sky.
    He's made friends with oyster fishermen
who take him out collecting. Specimens
    from tidal pools: grey, vanilla, smoky green.

'Procured from black rocks at Leith,
  a large Common Lumpfish, stranded. The ovaria
a great mass of rose-colour spawn.
  When dissected, as well as I could,

no intestinal worms. Free from disease. Eyes small –
  so probably does not inhabit deep seas?
Unusually for cartilaginous fish, the kidneys
  quite a way from the vertebrae.'

He gets no practice in dissection. His microscope
  is hopeless! He listens to a visitor, John Audubon,
on North American birds. Black windows gape
  in lecture halls like carbon wings. If he can't get on

with Medicine, will Father provide an allowance?
  At eighteen he falls in love – with marine invertebrates.
He reads a paper to a natural history society
  on his first discovery: the eggs of *Flustra*,

splodges of emerald tangle, combings
  of green hair at the tidal edge, are not a plant –
they're animal, they're larvæ! As for Medicine –
  he hates it. How can he tell them at home?

At Edinburgh Darwin joined the Plinian Society for Natural History and went to Natural History talks. He studied hard at medicine at first, but found the lectures boring.

BLISS CASTLE

The Mount, Shrewsbury, summer 1828.

'You care for nothing but shooting, rat-catching and dogs!
You'll be a disgrace to yourself and your family.'
His father is the largest man he'll ever know.

He's got to be a parson, plod through the Classics again
and read Divinity at Cambridge. So it's God
and Holy Orders? As well that, as anything. He accepts

the truth of Holy Writ. And the Creed, of course.
('It never struck me how illogical it was
to say I believed what I could not understand –

and what is, in fact, unintelligible.')
What matters most is shooting. The worst thing
that could happen would be getting an entry wrong

Maer Hall in Staffordshire was the seat of Josiah Wedgwood, son of the potter and brother of Darwin's dead mother. Uncle Jos's seven children included three girls: Charlotte, Fanny and Emma.

in his ledger of shot birds. He's nineteen
and the best fun is Bliss Castle, alias Maer Hall.
Lots of cousins, three girls, and a kind

sporty uncle. In the partridge and pheasant season
he keeps his boots beside the bed
not to lose thirty seconds of shooting-time.

THE CODDINGTON MICROSCOPE

I

HELD

Christ's College, Cambridge, 1829–31.

Stand, a moment, in the centre of these panels.
His room's empty now, being restored.
Just the mahogany table and carved doors –
leading, if you open them, one to a tiny bedroom,
one to a brick wall. A stone fireplace, chest-high,
just right for a gentleman to warm his backside

in icy weather. Outside are pale wood stairs
and steps to an upper floor
with a vertical iron bar to grab when drunk.
We're here. The mantle of antiquity, of *always.*
These rooms once belonged to William Paley!
The panels are bayonet geometries

For his course, required reading was *Natural Theology* (1802) by the philosopher and Christian apologist William Paley, later Archdeacon of Carlisle. By coincidence, Darwin had the rooms which Paley used at Christ's College. Darwin much admired Paley's *Natural Theology* and knew it practically by heart.

with Ionic capitals on top like a set
of watching owls. A Bible and Latin books un-
opened on the desk. 'I used to throw my gun
to my shoulder before the looking-glass
and fire with a cap on the nipple
at the flame of a candle held by a friend.

If my aim was accurate, the little puff of air
blew it out. There was a sharp crack!
When the Tutor passed below he thought I had a taste
for practising a horse-whip.'
He's twenty-one. Quite soon he'll be a parson
pursuing natural history part-time

but now the world is vivid, a bright rug
    of dark-hearted poppies. His collecting net
hangs from a pole like the dug
    of a breeding bitch. The circus of polished oak
reflects brass glitter on his Coddington's Microscope,
    the first real scientific instrument he's owned,

even more prized than his gun. He's friends
    with Botany and Geology professors; he competes
for favour at their lectures. He's in debt. He reads Paley –
    of course – and novels. He rides out to the Fens
to catch beetles. He dreams of a natural history expedition
    to Teneriffe, before he gets down to parsoning.

Let's walk him out to the jade lawn, scarlet geraniums
    and black stone walls (now cleaned and pale)
familiar, once, to Milton. Everything in its place:
    college history; the Laws of Nature and of God.
A great regard for understanding order
    stirs in him like a sleeping bird. A roc perhaps. Or a
                                                            phoenix.

Milton, who was intended for the priesthood like Darwin, had studied at Christ's College two centuries earlier (1625–32).

II

HE READS THAT THE MEMBRANE IN A GOLDFINCH EGG IS PROOF OF DIVINE DESIGN

Paley's 1802 argument, that design must have a designer, was revived in the 1980s as 'intelligent design'.

Evidences of the Existence and Attributes of the Deity,
Collected from Appearances of Nature
by William Paley. 'The Arteries might continue
shooting from their extremities indefinitely.
God could have done it without instruments or means!
But *how* instruments are made, *how* means become adapted –
that is where creative intelligence is seen!
God has prescribed limits to His power, to work His end
within them and so exhibit wisdom. He does the same with us.

You cannot lift your hand up to your head, simple as it seems,
without finding enough to be convinced of God's existence.
Reflect how many things are requisite to that performing!
How could all this muscle, nerve and glint of skin
be stitched together without intelligence?
From the white of egg, would anyone look
for feathers of a goldfinch? Who, that saw red streaks
shooting in the membrane which divides the yolk from white,
would guess they were destined for bones and limbs?'

III

ON ASKING A MUSEUM GUARD TO DRAW THE CURTAIN BEFORE TITIAN'S *VENUS*

Darwin often went to see paintings in the Fitzwilliam Museum. One he mentioned several times in later life was Titian's *Venus:* probably *Sleeping Venus,* then attributed to Padovanino, now labelled 'After Titian'. Though modelled on Giorgione's Dresden *Venus* (whose landscape and sky were finished by Titian), this may be a copy of a composition by Titian. In Darwin's time, though original works by an artist were valued as today, copies of his composition by other artists were not as sharply differentiated from their originals as they are now.

The Museum hung curtains over paintings of nudes to protect the modesty of women visitors.

Darwin's female cousins at Maer Hall were Charlotte, Fanny and Emma Wedgwood. He called Charlotte, the eldest, 'incomparable'.

Her sudden body. Bare vellum, horizontal:
    thighs crossed and lower knee flexed
below the upper calf. He knows the lines by heart:
    her fingers curving down and nestling – he can't see
the tips – in her crotch. One arm under her perfect head
    so the muscles of the under-shoulder melt

into her lower breast, the nipple looking at you
    like the only open eye. Except there's a soft,
bi-colour spaniel plonked on russet satin
    underneath. The dog sits sentinel, the only thing awake,
its wet gaze on you like a tongue. A curtain, not the real one
    the guard draws back but a painted drape,

protects her innocent circumflex of hair
    from a sleeping town behind. But her upper breast,
with that crisp little nipple, thrusts up into the landscape
    and deep inside his retina. Mysterious geology!
He wants to chamber it in his palm, shield
    it from any watcher hidden in that purple air.

The top-silhouetted tree pushes scratchy twigs –
    wiry, pubic – up from the horizon
into ochre cloud. This is what girls look like
    underneath! Behind the petalled skin and taffeta.
What the eyes behind those lowered eyelids
    see in the looking-glass. Charlotte, at Maer –

or the Owen sisters in their house of frolic!
    They call it 'The Forest'; *he* says 'Paradise'.
'Like any good Musselman, I am always thinking of it.
    Those Houris, though, are flesh and blood. Substantial.'
No lowered eyelids there! Fanny teases about beetles.
    He suspects she looks their names up in her father's library.

They take horses into the woods. She insisted, once,
    on trying to fire his gun – and fell, her soft
shoulder bruised by the recoil. She flirts, she pouts,
    they laugh a lot. 'I made a beast of myself,' she said,
'in the strawberry-beds.' Under the starch
    and flounce here's Venus, waiting for your touch.

Darwin spent a lot of time 'lovering', as he put it, with Fanny Owen, the younger of two sisters at a house near Shrewsbury called Woodhouse: hence the girls' nickname for it, 'The Forest'.

A DESPERATE WAY TO AVOID PAYING YOUR TAILOR

In summer 1831 Darwin passed his Divinity exams and in July went on a geology expedition to Wales with Sedgwick, Cambridge Professor of Geology.

His own work has revised the National Map!
    He's discovered there's no Old Red Sandstone
in the Vale of Clwyd.
    'A promising student of Geology'.

That'll help for Teneriffe (though not
    for entering the Church). 'How long
in the Tropics, without washing it,
    can you wear a shirt?' He's going home

for shooting, and lovering with Fanny Owen;
    but here's Fate, kicking at the door.

Henslow, Cambridge Professor of Botany, had discussed natural history with Darwin and knew he wanted to pursue it in the tropics. He had recommended Darwin for an Admiralty expedition and had written to Darwin to tell him.

Captain Fitzroy, relation of the Duke of Grafton,
    requires a gentleman companion, naturalist and savant,

for a survey of South America. Tierra del Fuego
    and back by the West Indies, starting in two months.
A professor, from Cambridge, is recommending *him*!
    'I immediately said I would go.' But no –

The Mount, Shrewsbury, August 1831.

'My idle son! Two universities, wasted
    in shooting, drinking, debts – and collecting insects!
Ships are like jails. Filthy, full of disease
    and brutal discipline! And what about shipwreck?

It would unfit you, on return, to be a clergyman.
    You have no experience in seafaring
and no time to prepare. And anyway
    you might not suit the Captain!'

Starry spaces of the world recede.
 'My Father, though he does not decidedly refuse,
gives such strong advice against
 that I should not be comfortable.'
He goes to Maer, to shoot. But Father knows

there won't be another chance like this
 and Cambridge dons aren't fools. 'If you can find
anyone of common sense who advises you to go
 I'll give consent.' At Maer they all say, *Go*!

His uncle drives him home. The dogrose,
 starry on August hedges along the white-dust road.
With Uncle there, Father OKs it – and Father has to pay.
 'I'd have to be deuced clever to get into debt on a boat!'

'But they all say you *are* very clever.' He's going to be a sailor –
 and there's a girl to leave behind.
'A pretty desperate way',
 says Fanny, 'to avoid paying your tailor.'

CHAPTER TWO

JOURNEY

1831–1836

. . . you see the lonely young man, his eyes fixed on facts and minute detail, sinking or sliding giddily off into the unknown.

Elizabeth Bishop, Letter to Anne Stevenson, 1964

SLIDING GIDDILY OFF INTO THE UNKNOWN

I

THE AWFULNESS OF PLYMOUTH

Laundering on a *ship*? His sisters mark his shirts 'Darwin'.
He packs *Paradise Lost*, the only book he'll slip
in his pocket wherever he goes. Plus his New Testament, in Greek,
a brace of pistols and a portable dissecting microscope.

Plymouth and Devonport, October–December 1831.

Captain Fitzroy gives him Lyell's *Geology*. The Captain's keen
on Natural History too; they all are, even the crew.
But now there's two, three months' delay. The cabins need
refitting, the little deck is raised. In the long provisioning

he starts a journal. The awfulness of Plymouth – and Devonport!
His hammock twists like an eel and spits him out. They set sail
in waves like fantasies of Jonah and then slink hugger-mugger
back to land. A letter, in his lodgings, from Fanny Owen.

The boat, H.M.S. *Beagle*, was only ninety feet long and the poop cabin, his and Fitzroy's main habitation for five years, was at least six inches under his height of six foot.

Her sister's married! 'How I wish you had been there. Pray,
my dear Charles, do write me one last adieu. How I wish
you had not this horrible Beetle taste. You cannot imagine
how I have *missed* you – how I long to see you again!'

In her letters, Fanny used 'Beetles' to stand for Darwin's interest in all natural history.

Christmas – the crew get drunk ashore. So more delay?
Black cilia sway inside him like a prophecy. They're off again
and he's sick, awash, in bits. He's one long see-saw
groan! The Captain beds him down on his own sofa.

They finally left on 27 December 1831. Darwin continued to be badly seasick throughout the five years' voyage.

II

CAT O' NINE TAILS

Shrieks above, on deck. That's one sailor lashed
by the cat, twenty-five times for Drunkenness.
Three strands of rope, unravelled into three
(a 'Trinity of Trinities' sets sinners on the path
to righteousness) and then replaited for a more
effective wound. Drum rolls – all hands to witness

Fitzroy told Darwin he was not as much of a martinet as some captains.

punishment. Silence as the tails are disentangled.
In the Bay of Biscay, the naturalist lies retching
on the floor, trying not to picture barbed knots
biting a cross on every spine and shoulderblade,
a glary scarlet scribble on open flesh. Again, again,
again. Thirty-one lashes for Neglect of Duty;

Disobeying Orders, thirty-four. Forty-four –
that's Drunkenness with Insolence. The Captain
says he must establish order from the start.
Leg irons on five more. Till we passed Teneriffe,
says the Captain's log, he was terribly sick.
'The misery', Charles tells his journal, 'is excessive.'

III

PLANKTON

January 1832. The *Beagle* was heading south through the North Atlantic towards the Cape Verde Islands.

The deck is dazzle, fish-stink, gauze-covered buckets.
  Gelatinous ingots, rainbows of wet flinching amethyst
  and flubbed, iridescent cream. All this
means he's better; and working on a haul of lumpen light.

Polyps, plankton, jellyfish. Sea butterflies, the pteropods.
  'So low in the scale of nature, so exquisite in their forms!
  You wonder at so much beauty – created,
apparently, for such little purpose!' They lower his creel

to blue pores of subtropical ocean. Wave-flicker, white
  as a gun-flash, over the blown heart of sapphire.
  Peacock eyes, beaten and swollen,
tossing on lazuline steel.

IV

LIKE GIVING TO A BLIND MAN EYES

January 1832, St Jago, Cape Verde Islands: Darwin's first glimpse of tropical vegetation.

He's standing in Elysium. Palm feathers, a green
   dream of fountain against blue sky. Banana fronds,
slack rubber rivulets, a canopy of waterproof tearstain
   over his head. Pods and racemes of tamarind.
Follicle, pinnacle; whorl, bole and thorn.

One of Darwin's great inspirations was the work on South America by Alexander von Humboldt, *Personal Narrative of Travels to the Equatorial Regions of the New Continent.*

'I expected a good deal. I had read Humboldt
   and was afraid of disappointment.'
What if he'd stayed at home? 'How utterly vain
   such fear is, none can tell but those who have seen
what I have today.' A small rock off Africa –

alone with his enchantment. So much and so unknown.
   Like taking a newborn baby in your arms. 'Not only the grace
of forms and rich new colours: it's the numberless –
   & confusing – associations rushing on the mind!'
He walks through hot damp air

and tastes it like the breath of earth, like blood.
   He is possessed by chlorophyll. By the calls of unknown birds.
He wades into sea and scares an octopus. It puffs black hair
   at him, turns *red* – as hyacinth – and darts for cover.
He sees it watching him. He's discovered

something wonderful! He tests it against coloured card
   and the sailors laugh. They know that girly blush!
He feels a fool – but look, he's touched tropical Volcanic rock
   for the first time. And Coral on its native stone.
'Often at Edinburgh have I gazed at little pools

of water left by tide. From tiny Corals of our shores
I pictured larger ones. Little did I know how exquisite,
still less expect my hope of seeing them to come true.
Never, in my wildest castles of the air, did I imagine this.'
Lava must once have streamed on the sea-floor here,

baking shells to white hard rock. Then a subterranean force
pushed everything up to make an island.
Vegetation he's never seen, and every step a new surprise.
'New insects, fluttering about still newer flowers. It has been
for me a glorious day, like giving to a blind man eyes.'

V

LAVENDER LIGHT IN A LEAP YEAR

To a person fond of natural history, such a day as this will bring a deeper pleasure than he can hope ever to experience again.

Darwin, *Journal of Researches into the Natural History and Geology of the Countries Visited during the Voyage of H.M.S. Beagle*, 1845

On 29 February 1832, in Bahia (now Salvador), Brazil, Darwin took his first steps in untouched tropical forest.

He's on his own in pristine rainforest. 'Delight
is too weak a word for how a naturalist,
alone the first time with all this, must feel.'
(Little does he know of the letter, already written,
he's going to find at Rio. Fanny Owen
hasn't hung around.) First oddity – the guttural silence.
Then the succulents. Bromeliads, parasite
plants he's never seen. Tree ferns! Jade wagon wheels
eighty feet up like jugglers' saucers on a pole.

Bristle of orchid leaves on every black branch
like green flames over Bibles.
Botanical forms gyrate and pour
through rivers of otherworld bark
and a wrestling musculature of pure
live wood. This churchy breathing dark –
surely he lived here as a boy, or before he was born.
He's a revenant, a sleepwalker. The lavender light
is dim, like underwater. One ray, a lost firework,

a jewel-finger through stained glass.
    Pale trees of drizzly twilit bloom
with epiphytes at their throat, like muezzin
platforms on the minarets he's only seen
    in illustrations. Leaves of all textures that a leaf
could be: palm, fluff, prickle, matte and plume;
bobbled; shaggy plush. A thousand shades
    of ochre, silver, emerald, smoky brass.
He's walking into every dream he's ever seen:

tasselled seedpods, trefoil, nodule;
    shrapnel of decaying trees like giant
columns of a fallen temple, their gold-bone
mossy architraves upwelted with lianas.
    Creepers – and a strangler ficus – crafting their way
to the light. Relationships! And inside, who knows
what amphibia, mammals, reptiles?
    Somewhere in this dreamtangle are tree frog,
rattlesnake, toucan, *fer de lance*. Sudden pistol shots

above – no – slashing raindrops, plump as eggs,
    vaulting from a sky he cannot see,
contiguous as a sheet of falling glass. Under a Jack
and the Beanstalk tree (a pillar of melted amber),
    he leans on slippery roots like fins veloured
in moss, stippled pink where the moss has rubbed.
Like tubers – or a tree-gland – hard as mumps.
    Forget the dense-ply canopy: at once
there's a torrent, blackening the trunk.

VI

A QUARREL IN BAHIA HARBOUR

Bahia, March 1832. Slavery was abolished in England in 1772 and slave trading in British colonies in 1807. But this exacerbated trading by other nations and Portugal continued transporting Africans to Brazil. Darwin was horrified. All his family had campaigned for abolition; his grandfather Josiah Wedgwood made for the abolition movement a medallion saying, 'Am I Not a Man and a Brother?' In 1832 Darwin and his sisters were waiting impatiently for the British government to emancipate slaves in British colonies: the law was passed in August that year.

He heard how it felt to walk in jungle first
from John Edmonstone. His teacher, the freed slave.
        Now, in this city on a pink-lit bay, lightning
snaps beneath his feet. He sees the slaves
themselves. Auctions. Blows. Humanity betrayed.

His waistcoat crackles with static. In the marl
of a river crossing, to make sure the ferry-pilot,
    a tall black slave, knows where he needs to go,
he explains a little louder – as you do –
and waves his hands. Terrified, the fellow shuts his eyes.

'He thought I was in a passion and meant to strike!
I shall never forget my shame and my surprise
        at seeing a great, powerful man afraid
even to ward off a blow
directed, he thought, at his face. He was trained

to degradation lower than the most helpless animal!'
But Captain Fitzroy thinks different.
He's seen a plantation-owner ask his slaves
if they *wanted* to be free – 'And they said "No!"'
Does saying it to their master's face prove *anything*?

'We cannot live together if you doubt my word!'
The Captain bangs out of the cabin
and curses him, on deck, all evening.
Will he have to leave the boat? Fitzroy sends apologies.
They never speak of slavery again.

Fitzroy and Darwin shared the captain's living quarters. Their worst quarrel was over slavery. Fitzroy later changed his views.

THE FLOWER GARDEN AT MAER

I

HE REPLIES TO HIS FIRST LETTER FROM HOME

Letter to his sister Caroline, Rio de Janeiro, 6 April 1832.

'This is my life as a Sailor. I really am becoming one.
Knowing ropes & how to put the ship about.
I like bare living on blue water. But I bargain
with Aeolus! I implore him to keep the sea quiet –

my poor stomach was only just able to save
its credit, leaving Bahia. We lay to last night. The Captain
wanted us to see Rio Harbour, & be ourselves seen,
in broad daylight. We opened our eyes

to mountains as rugged as Wales but clothed in evergreen
and the light form of the Palm. A City gaudy with towers
and Cathedrals – and a vast blue bay
studded with men of war and flags of every nation.

We came along the Admiral's ship in first-rate style.
Beautiful discipline! In the midst of our Tactics
the bundle of letters arrived. I could see yours –
from December – so long ago! "Send 'em below,"

came the order. "Every fool is neglecting his duty!"
When I got them, though the view was glorious
in bright sun, and our little ship working like a fish,
away I rushed, to feast on reading you!

The thought of home made the present more exciting –
but that feeling soon dispersed. *Three* weddings!
Even Charlotte! I see the flower garden at Maer . . .
And Fanny Owen! Melting with tenderness I cry,

"My dearest Fanny".' ('I cannot bear to part with you',
she'd said, 'so long.') 'I vote this marrying a bore.
I like unmarried women better. At this rate
I have no chance for my dream of some green parsonage.'

The letters waiting at Rio included one from Darwin's cousin Charlotte Wedgwood saying that she (and coincidentally her brother too) was getting married; and another from his sister Catherine, saying that a few days after the *Beagle* sailed, Fanny Owen had accepted a proposal from another man.

II

IN THE SERAGLIO

From April to June 1832 Darwin rented a cottage on Botofogo Bay outside Rio, collecting, exploring and learning the tropics. The walks he took here were among the most vivid of his whole journey.

He lies in the hot blind kitchen of night
   in his cottage on Botofogo Bay, listening
to sleepy begin-calls of birds. He can feel
   jungle press the house around him.

'A forest is a gold mine to a Naturalist.'
   The live hush – rustle – reverence.
He feels walls of his life dropping away.

You need people who know
   the broken trails, sudden pits underfoot,
and the animals. Capybara, jaguar, agouti.

The canopy closes overhead like a cathedral;
   or how a Turkish Bath might feel
in Babylon. 'As a Sultan in a Seraglio
   I am becoming quite hardened to beauty.'

III

ANOTHER LETTER FROM A SISTER

From Darwin's younger sister Catherine, written at The Mount, Shrewsbury, 25 July 1832.

'I hope you find Fanny *Wedgwood* free
when you return. A nice, invaluable little Wife
she'd be. I will not promise though.
Another Clergyman is paying her attention

but such a fat and horrid man
I cannot think she means to have him.
When she admired flowers in the greenhouse
he said he had a prettier one and pulled out

from his pocket a paper on which Fanny –
weeks before – had scrawled a flower!
Emma was by – choking! Laughing at the man's
odd manner; and Fanny, so amazed!'

Maer Hall, Staffordshire, August 1832.

When he reads this in Buenos Aires,
Fanny Wedgwood will have died
from an inflammatory disease
with Emma, her little sister, by her side.

LEAVING BRAZIL

I

THE THUMBSCREWS OF RIO

Augustus Earle was the artist on the *Beagle*.

'Mr Earle has seen a stump of the joint wrenched off
by the thumbscrew so often kept in a family house.'
A simple vice, with studs on interior surfaces.
The thumb placed in and slowly crushed.
Faces so close they smell each other's breath.

'If I hear a distant scream, I remember a house
where I heard most pitiable moans and I suspected
some poor slave was being tortured
but was powerless to remonstrate. I lived opposite
an old lady who crushed the fingers of her female slaves;

I stayed in a home where a young mulatto was reviled,
beaten and persecuted every hour,
enough to break the spirit of the lowest animal.
I have seen a boy, six or seven, struck thrice
with a whip on his naked head before I could interfere

for having handed me a glass of water not quite clean.
I saw his father tremble at a single glance
from his master's eye. This day we have finally
left the shores of Brazil. I thank God I shall never see
a slave-country again.'

19 August 1832.

II

REMEMBERING MILTON IN THE NIGHT AT SEA

. . . through the gloom were seen
Ten thousand Banners rise into the Air
With Orient Colours waving . . .
Milton, *Paradise Lost*, Book 1, 544–46

'The night pitch dark. The whole sea luminous.
Every part of water which by day is seen as foam
glowed with pale light. The vessel drove before her bows

Written on the voyage from Bahia Blanca to Montevideo, 23 October 1832.

two billows of liquid phosphorus. Her wake was a milky train.
As far as the eye reached, the crest of every wave was bright;
& from the reflected light the sky – just above horizon –

not so utterly dark as the rest of the Heavens.
Impossible to behold this plain of matter, as it were melted
& consumed by heat, without remembering Milton!'

RED SNOW

I

CHRISTMAS AT PORT DESIRE

Primeval forests undefaced by the hand of man . . . of Brazil where the powers of life predominate . . . of Tierra del Fuego where death and decay prevail. Both are temples filled with the varied productions of the God of Nature. No one can stand unmoved in these solitudes without feeling there is more in man than the mere breath of his body.

Darwin, *Journal of Researches into the Natural History and Geology of the Countries Visited during the Voyage of H.M.S. Beagle*, 1845

Patagonia, Argentina, December 1833.

In Montevideo Conrad Martens replaced Augustus Earle as the *Beagle*'s artist.

South American 'ostriches' are actually rheas. The men ate Martens's rhea, which was unusually small. Darwin assumed it was a young one. But he kept the bones, skin and feathers, which were later reassembled in London as representative species of the smaller rhea, *Rhea darwinii* – named after a man who had eaten it. Darwin greatly enjoyed telling this story afterwards.

On the hot trek inland, looking for water, he walks
twenty miles further than Fitzroy and has fever for two days.
Puerto Deseado, wrong side of the globe.
'We saw a field solid with snow-white salt.'
He shoots a guanaco, a hundred and seventy pounds,
for Christmas lunch. He's been away too long.

'Mr Martens shot an ostrich.' Bog-blown grass: a sepia
like fraying chiffon. 'All here is desolation.
One reflects how many centuries it has thus been,
how many more will thus remain. Yet in this scene,
without one bright object, there is high pleasure
which I can neither comprehend nor explain.'

II

ALGAE FROM THE ARCTIC

On high trails, the mules leave scarlet dints in snow
as if their feet had bled. He scoops up the wet red
and rubs it. It isn't the claret dust of porphyry, blown
from peaks of the Peuquenes. Nor granite
from the blue-roan Portillo ridge. No –

Cordillera, Chile, March 1835.

none of this heart-sweeping geology of Cordillera,
the ashy wind, guanaco flocks
and level-soaring condors,
which has bewitched him on this jaunt
to the interior. (He's done so many, now.)

'I felt glad I was by myself. Bright-coloured rocks,
profound valleys, heaped ruins
and wild broken forms – like watching
a thunderstorm or hearing in full Orchestra
a chorus from *The Messiah*.'

In the microscope, ruby specks glow
in ice the mules have squashed. 'Like eggs
of small molluscous animals.' Or mini ticks
full of blood. With Covington, he posts them off
to Cambridge, to be identified as algae from the Arctic.

In spring 1833, Darwin had taught the *Beagle*'s cabin boy, Syms Covington, to shoot. Subsequently he hired Covington, with the Captain's blessing, as his personal servant and assistant.

III

GIANT BUGS OF THE PAMPAS

Luxan, south of Mendoza, Chile, spring 1835.

Horses and guns, like at home. The ostriches run,
you can see them for miles, swaying the masts
of their necks in a bustle of black and white skirts.
Shadows of enormous eggs, abandoned on the plain.
Twilight. A just-painted fresco, a melt-mist of dun
and blue-rose. Men laughing. They are young,
they are galloping, loving it, little twisty runs
of sweat in the wind on their hair. The strange
gaucho saddle. A moon above pale pampas,
a slice of silver gristle. And company at night
as Covington builds a fire and stacks the specimens.

'Most disgusting, to feel soft wingless insects,
about an inch long, called *Chinches* or *Benchuga*,
soft & numerous on all parts of your person, gorged
with your blood!' *Triatoma infestans*, the kissing bug –
a handsome yellow-orange, trimmed with stripy chevrons
like edging-braid at the bottom of a curtain –
drawn to our skin by heat sensors in antennae
and pheromones left on us invisibly
by earlier such predators. Triatomines hide
in cushions, mattresses and wall cracks,
emerging to eat at night. A proboscis, a thin needle

coated with anticoagulant and anaesthetic, pierces skin
        and sucks and swells. The engorging abdomen
triggers peristalsis. Faeces inject a protozoan,
        Trypanosoma cruzi, into the wound
and into your bloodstream. The microbe hunters haven't got going
        yet. (Louis Pasteur's thirteen.) The bacteria
that will afflict this Charles and his unborn children
        are life-forms as occult as Kabbalah or that other
secret scripture DNA: a hidden barcode
        invisible as a string of fireflies
sleeping on a leaf-edge in the pre-dusk blue of day.

'Good to experience everything once.' He's an adept
        beetle-hunter. 'I caught a very empty one.'
They place it on a barrel in the hut. A ring
        of stubbled chins. Owl eyes in candlelight.
He holds his finger out. Come in Chagas' Disease, endemic
        to South America. The symptoms are fever, headache
and malaise; aching joints, a swollen liver, spleen and eyes;
        neurological, gastro-intestinal and cardiac damage.
Often fatal – and lasts all your life. 'The bold insect was out
        with its sucker and began to draw blood. No pain.
Curious to watch it, in less than ten minutes, change size.'

Chagas' Disease is endemic to South America. The illness Darwin suffered from 1839 for the rest of his life may have been due, at least partly, to Chagas' Disease.

ON NOT THINKING ABOUT VARIATION IN TORTOISE-SHELL

He tells them of a new World and new kind of Creature to be created.
Milton, *Argument* to *Paradise Lost*, Book I

Galapagos Islands, September 1835.

Pure volcano. A mantle of hot bare rock. 'Nothing could be less
inviting. A broken field of black basaltic lava
thrown into most rugged waves and crossed
by fissures.' Lava tubes, tuff cones and bright,
red-orange crabs. A land iguana! One saffron
leathery elbow, powdery as lichen, sticking out

like a man doing press-ups while leering at the sand.
The marine iguana – 'Hideous! An imp of darkness.
On Albermarle they seem to grow to a larger size.'
Young sea lions nip their tails for fun and fling them in the air
like cats with mice. To eat them? No – nothing here,
except one hawk, is carnivore; and none afraid of Man.

Until he was back in London, Darwin did not realize the full significance of animal variation on different islands. He did see, at once, variation between mockingbirds on the first and second islands. That realization was the key to everything that followed, above all the proof of species change. But he failed to label his finch specimens with the name of the island each came from and later asked to see the finches of Fitzroy and Covington, who brought back their own birds and *had* labelled them.

Look – giant tortoises! 'Travelling eagerly, their necks
outstretched, to springs. I tried riding on their backs
but found it hard to balance! The colony's Vice-Governor
told us he knew which island any shell came from
because they differ. I did not for some time
pay this enough attention. I never dreamed

that islands sixty miles apart, made of the same stone,
of nearly equal height in the same climate,
could have different tenants.' Fast forward twenty years
and you see him write of this scatter-burst of rock in open sea,
'We seem brought near that mystery of mysteries,
the first appearance of new beings on the earth.'

CHAPTER THREE

CITY

1837–1838

NOTEBOOK B

I

HE FINDS HIS OWN DEFINITION OF GRANDEUR

'What a magnificent view one can take of the world!'
    He has rooms in Great Marlborough Street. Covington
helps him move in. A Queen has ascended a throne.
He bowls across the city, three notebooks on the go.
'Events in astronomy, modified by others – unknown –
    cause changes in geography and climate. These induce
changes in the organic zone. By changing, they affect

each other too. Their bodies keep perfect
    in themselves by certain laws of harmony.
Instincts alter – reason is born. All living forms
have to adapt.' What we take on a journey.
What we bring back. 'So, from a period just short of eternity
    till now, the world fills like an expanding well with myriads
of different forms. What grandeur in this view of world!

Far better than the thought (proceeding, surely,
    from a cramped imagination) that God,
warring against the laws He set up, in organic nature,
created the rhinoceros of Java and Sumatra!'
He's in a rush – audacious – dangerous.
    Boundaries drop away. If living beings change!
'And man – from monkeys?'

March 1838.

Returning to England, October 1836, Darwin distributed his *Beagle* collections to mammal, bird and fossil experts, and began writing up the geology and his Journal. In 1837 he became a Fellow of the Geological Society at Somerset House and in 1838 its Secretary. He moved to London with Covington, who was his servant and assistant until 1839, when he emigrated to Australia. They continued to correspond.

From 1837 on, Darwin filled a series of alphabetically named notebooks with 'mental rioting'. They were his life. He reassessed in them everything he had thought about the voyage and added new thoughts. Notebook B was for evolution ('transformism' he called it then). He backed up his species speculations with a diagram: a tree of life with ancestors at the bottom and modern species at the top.

His hairdresser in Great Marlborough Street
    takes an interest in pedigree hounds! Ask him about
the principles of breeding. 'Is it polite
to say that ever since Silurian times, God's made
a succession of vile molluscous animals
    in infinite variation? How beneath the dignity
of Him who said, *Let there be light!*'

II

ON THE PROPAGATION OF MISTLETOE

Fountain of the river-god. Water like a shadow of glass
on milky stone. Ribbed brass of the doorknob
at Somerset House. Why do two rhea species
divide the pampas? 'Taxonomy of past
animals – fossils – a clue?' Chill parquet corridors.
A stone sphinx on the stairs. 'I'm not denying laws!
But sexual reproduction is the driving force.'

Jolt of a carriage up Strand. The river's cindery flush
whipped to meringue by the wind. 'Who'd have thought
the intestine of a thrush enough to ensure
propagation in common mistletoe? As for a wife –
heaven knows if she exists, whether I shall ever catch
that most interesting specimen of vertebrates
or be able to feed her if caught.'

In March 1837 John Gould, Darwin's bird expert for his *Beagle* specimens, told Darwin that the Galapagos finches were an entirely new group; and each a different species; that mockingbirds on different islands were different species; and the southern rhea was a different species from the northern. Darwin suddenly saw a vital parallel – between geographical relationships between living species and temporal relationships between living and extinct species. This led him to his concept of 'transmutation of species': everything, including human beings, was part of one ancestral chain. From now on this was the undisclosed hub of all his thought.

III

THE FREE WILL OF AN OYSTER

Probably some error in the argument here. Should be grateful if pointed out.

Darwin, *Notebook M*, 1838

Lurcher puppies, brown and gold, playing in the straw
of a farmyard. Ears, teeth and tails. The individual
in society. Tussle, flight; invention, fight.

'It cannot be doubted that they have free will.
If they, then all animals – even an oyster:
whose free will must result from the limits of shell,
pulp, valve. Free will is to mind what chance

is to matter, changing the body's arrangements.
So may free will make changes, too, in Man.'
And the mind, belvedere of the body?
'Beyond doubt, part of the process.'

No deity, no lutes of paradise. Only the smell of tall grass,
tissue adaptive as light from a star
and quick cells vivid to change in the struggle for life.

NOTEBOOK M

Notebooks M and N were for 'Metaphysics with Morals & Speculations on Expression': the basis of Darwin's later work on human and animal psychology.

Painfully and disagreeably human.
Queen Victoria

The first ape seen in London Zoo was Tommy in 1835: a chimpanzee dressed in Guernsey frock and sailor hat. Jenny the orang-utang went on show (also in a frock) in November 1837. From March 1838 Darwin paid her several visits. The Queen saw a second Jenny in 1839, after the first Jenny died.

Raw blush of flamingos, burning the air. Small birds
pecking gravel beyond black bars. Invisible lions
roaring at feeding-time. Gibbons, each a black crucifix

splayed on the wire, duet with each other. An elephant
sways up the path. Here is the man, his big nose –
and his eyes, always upon her, flapping their wings.

*

Where was she caught? Sumatra? Borneo?
Her arms are brandy-snap sugar; her face
    a prune-colour damask. 'With her teeth
she nipped a pellet from the straw. Not knowing
what to do with it, she opened my hand
    and tipped it in like a child.' Moustache
of ginger flame. Speckled pores
of sunset round the eyes. 'She kissed
    her keeper's cheek.'

Her mouth is a pendulous thong. The eyes
merry brown glass like a carousel horse
    and wise as an antique doll.
'When she knows she's done wrong
she hides for shame – or maybe in fear.
    When she thinks she'll be whipped
she covers herself in straw.' Feelings appear
in her labial muscle, the treacly red haw
    of her eye. Where are the roots of morality?

*

A male orang who joined Jenny was unwell when Darwin saw him.

In 1838 most naturalists in London ridiculed the suggestion of shared ancestry between apes and humans. Seeing apes in clothes, using spoons and drinking tea, upset some people but did not make them question the moral and mental uniqueness of human beings. 'In nothing does it trench upon the moral or mental provinces of man,' said one newspaper.

'Wrist dangling, like a man who has given up
again and again. One palm supporting his head
like a man beyond measure fatigued.' (Or seasick,
perhaps?) 'Our affections are animal!
They result from us being social, like deer.'
Listless cinnamon hair. Hurt stare
from dull faraway eyes. But the facial grooves
reflect his own. This is the recognized Urdu
of human expression. Biblical; a voice
from a well; a spark of the planet's first fire
set free from a fossil. 'So why not the feelings, too?'

*

September 1838, with Jenny.

Splash of yellow on green in the Regent's Park trees.
He brings verbena, a bag of peppermint. A mouth organ,
a looking-glass. 'She listened to tunes with great attention
and readily put the instrument to her own mouth.
She seemed to relish the taste of mint
and scent of verbena. She was astonished at the mirror –

staring in every way, upside down and even behind
with most steady surprise.' Red grass of her jowls,
russet half-moons beneath her eyes. Her split-rubber lips.
'She took bread from a visitor, tilting her brow
at the keeper, to see whether this was allowed.

Man thinks himself, in his arrogance, a great work
and worthy a Deity's glance. More humble –
and true, I'd assert – to think him created, not bandbox new
but slowly. From this. From the animals.
Once you have granted one species may change
to another, the whole fabric totters and falls.'

THE TIGER IN KENSINGTON GARDENS

Everything I thought or read was made to bear directly on what I had seen or was likely to see. This habit of mind was continued during the five years of my voyage. I feel sure that it was this training which has enabled me to do whatever I have done in science.

Darwin, *Autobiography*

The forms are themselves. They do not change with the changing light
    but unfurl in the mind. They swirl and settle new
        in the kaleidoscope in his head

attentive as an extra eye with nothing, now, to numb
    or harden sight. 'Much imagination in every view. August 1838.
        My pleasure in Kensington Gardens often excited

by seeing a tree as a great – compound – animal, united
    in a manner most wonderful – & mysterious.
        Admiring a banyan in India

if a tiger stalked across the plain behind
    how feeling would be ignited –
        how the scenery would rise!'

WHAT IS AN EMOTION?

I

THE DEVIL AS BABOON

Darwin began reading Malthus's *Essay on the Principle of Population* on 28 September 1838. In it he found 'a theory by which to work', which led him to the concept of natural selection.

Two lamps lit. He's finishing Malthus. Shadows dance
in the room like a scritch of black rain.
'All forms compete against others for means of their life.
Nature's forms do *not* demonstrate benevolence, divine
or otherwise! The principle of population is strife.

Disease and pain in the world – and they talk of perfection?'
We are alone with our biology. 'New life is born
from famine, extinction, death.' Covington draws a curtain
against crêpe smog. Granite sparks
in the pavement outside. Applewood spits on the hearth.

'The human mind is shaped by its animal past. Every species
enshrines its ancestors in that stub of a tail at the end
of the spine. But instincts, desires – these have a history too.
Aggression, anger and revenge
once preserved us. But conditions have changed.

We try to restrain these passions that derive from our descent.'
Raindrops through soot. Iron heels and hooves
rattle below like barrels clattering down cellar steps.
'The origin of man is now proved.' The animal in us
has the loudest tunes. 'Our grandfather is Satan – in the form
of a baboon!'

— II —

WHY HERMAPHRODITE IS SECOND-BEST

'Blushing! Chameleon, octopus and human. Why do joy
    and other feelings make even grown-ups cry?'
London streets filthy. The rooms uncomfortable.
    He feels often ill. A chorus of soot-flakes
sifts down on the windowsill. 'What goes through
    a man's mind when he says that he loves?
Is it blind, something like sexual? Affection is the effect
    of physical organization. As you can hardly doubt

watching Caroline's dog, at Shrewsbury, with her puppy.'
    Autumn. Chill city ruckus outside. He looks at his cuff,
stained and frayed. He starts a new page. 'Inherited traits,
    patristic feather and bone
would never be pooled, species would never form to share
    the social instinct, if they created offspring
hermaphroditically, alone.' Like charcoal, sinking to the fire
    where it was born. 'What you need is a pair.'

III

WHITENESS AT THE END OF A DISTANT VIEW

In 1838, Darwin was working with different zoological experts on his animal and fossil specimens. He edited their findings in *The Zoology of the Voyage of H.M.S. Beagle*, which he published in nineteen numbers, 1838–43. In 1838 he was also writing up the geology himself.

Bad headaches. Agitated. Tired. The strain of editing.
'I have often thought of the viscosity of glacial ice,
the enormous momentum of great icebergs and their power
to make grooves.' Not sleeping well. 'Can a man like me
ever find relaxation and a home?' He's visiting a contributor.

Reptiles, amphibia; habits and ranges; fossil *Mammalia*.
'Sometimes I see ahead a cottage of rusty brick
hiding in light green, and before it some white thing
like a petticoat – which drives the forms of granite clean
out of my head in the most unphilosophical manner.'

IV

THE BALANCE SHEET

Against

'Freedom to go where I please. Conversation of clever men July 1838.
at clubs. Choice of society: and little of it . . . No one to interfere
with solitude I need. Not forced to visit relatives, or bend
in every trifle. Whoever she is might hate London!

Children are anxiety, responsibility, expense.
Not so much money for books. There could be misrule
in the house. Quarrelling, even. Banished to country,
unable to read in the evening, becoming fat indolent fool.

Eheu! I should never know French, see America, go up
in a balloon! But – no children, no second life, no one to care
about me in old age. Why continue working all day with no
sympathy from near & dear?' But who? Who would it be?

For

'A constant companion and friend in old age.
An object to be loved & played with. Better than dog.
Children, if it please God. A home –
and someone to care for it. Female chat

good for one's health. Charm of music, perhaps.
Terrible loss of my time –
but my God picture a whole life spent like a neuter bee
working in smoke and grime

of a London house all day alone!
Then think of a nice soft wife on a sofa, looking at me
with a good fire and books. Look at dingy
Gt. Marlbro' St! Marry, marry, marry, Q.E.D.'

V

HIS FATHER ADVISES

Shrewsbury, 1838.

The church, where his mother is buried. The Quarry Pool.
The kennels. 'Conceal your religious doubts
from any future wife. I have seen
the extreme misery they cause. Things go on pretty well
till one of the pair falls ill. Then the wife
suffers, doubting her husband's salvation.
Causing suffering, likewise, in him.'

VI

HOW DO SPECIES RECOGNIZE THEIR MATE?

How an animal distinguishes a potential mate from others of similar species is not a question Darwin addressed; though later in *The Descent of Man* he did discuss visual factors in choice of a mate within a species.

Take frogs. Many different species lie about in wet fluorescence,
torn scraps of silk in the silt of a single pond.
To pick mates of their own species, they make themselves distinct
in tiny ways; like trembling at a particular frequency
or pulse rate. In birds, the variation's greater. Say, a courtship dance.
They meet, spread wings, display those peacock eyes,
that special patch of feathers, a flash or bar of black,
gold, iridescent blue, so the neurons, synaptic terminals
and brain may recognize the *I belong with you*.

VII

THE GATEKEEPER

London, 9 November 1838.

A railway. Nothing to climbing the Cordillera.
A ticket to Staffordshire. He feels white-hot
with holes where his stomach should be,
as if trying to shit the prickles of a star.
He's got a headache. He must be, surely, ill.

Everything's new-designed. The mahogany
frame of the ticket-seller's window.
The man, an embossed badge on his new cap
flickering, slides a ticket over the brass sill
like the gatekeeper to a volcano.

VIII

THE HOUR BEFORE SUNDAY SCHOOL

At Maer Hall, on 11 November 1838, he proposed to Emma Wedgwood, his first cousin.

He feels precarious, like facing a brass whip
of lightning over the sea. What is a self?
A glass you can't climb out of. The bottom of a crater.

In a moment she'll be off to teach the village children.
Everyone wants her. She's beyond his reach.
He's ugly as well as ill.

The carpet in the drawing-room, where he's always felt at home,
pours up into his soul. She stands by the window
in a paste of yellow light from the morning's tongue.

He studies the surface of what he can cling to
like a wounded angel, wondering how pieces of theory
fall at him out of a box. He keeps shaking the box.

Everything about him feels alive and terrified.
He stands at the end of his shadow, thinking what to say next,
looking at nature foaming between them

in the pool of his question. All these liquid metaphors
for feeling and for mind! And this long-known floaty abyss
of not being, ever being, all his life, handsome enough.

CHAPTER FOUR

EMMA

1838–1851

THE MOST TRANSPARENT MAN I EVER SAW

I

TROPICAL FOREST

Perhaps, after all, the angel was not wounded.
Kingdoms of his life rearranged themselves like cloud
after a storm. He felt washed open – an oyster
cleansed of grit. Marine metaphors flowed over him
as when he paced the deck of the little lone *Beagle*
at night. He felt loose, like a runaway cartwheel
bouncing from the heights into a valley
of violet oak trees. They stood
silent in the drawing-room, surprised.
She'd be engineer of all his happiness. Bees
shifted honey-bags up his spine. He was roses
burning alive, and she was the haze
above tropical forest plus the unfathomed riches
within. Like giving to a blind man eyes.

II

SHE DIDN'T THINK HE CARED

Emma Wedgwood, 1838.

'I was glad he was not too sure of being accepted. I went
immediately to the village school but found after an hour
  I'd taught the children nothing, was turning into an idiot
and so came away. He is the most transparent man I ever saw
  and most affectionate. Every word expresses his real thought.
But he is so fond of us all at Maer, so demonstrative
  in his manner, I did not think it meant anything. The week
I spent in London, earlier, I felt sure he did not care
about me. He was very unwell. That was all.'

III

HE IGNORES HIS FATHER'S ADVICE

Maer Hall, December 1838.

Milton, *Paradise Lost*, 1.22.

Her face pale as vaulting in the Cordillera church
where he read Milton one morning alone. *What in me
is dark, illumine*. He's trying to heft his doubt
about Christian Revelation. The leaves of his life
are gossiping around him. He accepts Christian morality,
of course! He stares at a quiff of feather on her skirt.

He'd like, he really would, to believe in afterlife
and the promise of Salvation. A sudden flush
like coral cloud in eastern sky, a photochemical exchange
on the face he's known since he was small, marks passage
of the prayer that must be moving in her mind
like dolphins underwater. *God grant he change*.

He's sure, now, morality has organic origin.
'Luckily there's no doubt how we ought to act.'
He stares at a caryatid holding up the mantelpiece.
He's known this, too, all his life. 'As for salvation:
other people find the arguments convincing.'
Their eyes meet – there's that, at least. 'I can't.'

IV

A PATH AROUND A LAKE

Maer Hall, December 1838.

She's merry, liberal, untidy, thirty-one. Grey-green eyes;
 and hair the colour of dry tobacco. She's turned six
good men down. On the piano her touch is crisp
 (she had lessons from Chopin once) but her slow
movements too *allegro*. Beside Fanny (two
sisters never apart, a two-who-thought-as-one) she was a dragoness
 at archery. They danced the cotillion in Rome, saw *La Cenerentola*
 at the opera in Venice. A quick ear for language – and humbug.
Fluent Italian. 'Affectionate, unaffected and, young as she is,
 full of the old times at heart.' She nurses her mother (once so
charming) in dementia. 'Epileptic fits,' they say. 'A clouded brain.'

A description of Emma in 1840, after she married, by the novelist Maria Edgeworth.

Now she's alone, watching silver birches dance
 in the wind beside St Peter's Church where she'll become
a wife. Winter cloud like dimpled tallow. *Now we see*
 in a glass, darkly. Then, face to face. Now I know in part
but then I'll know, even as I am known.
This is the window where she watched the park, through leaded
 diamonds, with Fanny. She does not go on about faith
 but she is liable, now, to interleave pages of her Bible
with notes for future prayer. 'Hope for reunion after death –
 mainstay of future happiness.' Sequins of orange lichen
on greystone balustrade, and on portico steps

1 Corinthians 13.12.

above the flower garden, where they sat on summer
evenings long ago. White sheep on the faraway hill, below
the woods' dark hieroglyph, are salt upturned on baize.
When small, they picnicked at the Roman fort,
cantered ponies across heath and rowed across the lake
to the farther shore: a journey to world's end on water wide
as ocean. *Who believeth in him will not perish* John 3.16.
but have everlasting life. Seven years ago,
when Fanny died, she tried to concentrate
on meeting her again, in Paradise.
'Separation such as this', she wrote then, in her journal,

'must bring the next world nearer.' She sees a fish rise,
breaking the skin of the lake. Scorings on the rim
of a potter's wheel. Circles widening on glass. *The natural man* 1 Corinthians 2.14.
receiveth not things of the Spirit. They are foolishness
to him. Neither can he know them, for they are spiritually discerned.
'It is foolish perhaps. But now we belong, my own
dear Charlie, to each other, I cannot help being open
with you. Melancholy thoughts keep generally out of my head
but since you are gone, some sad ones have forced themselves in.
I know we feel the same about right and wrong.
But our opinions on the most important thing

1 Corinthians 2.5.

are very different.' *Your faith should stand in the power*
of God, not the wisdom of man. 'My reason says honest
conscientious doubt cannot be a sin
but it would be a painful void. Religion is an affair of the heart
not the intellect. This is a whim of mine: if you would read
Our Saviour's farewell to His disciples. The part
of the New Testament I love best.' She looks at the sandy path
where they used to run as children round the lake.
He'll read the thing, never doubt it. Then?
'Though, I can hardly tell why,
I don't wish you to give me your opinion about it.'

— V —

COLD WATER THROWN ON THE HEAD

He's looked for lodgings for them both all day. December 1838.
Before the feast of Passover, Jesus knew his hour was come Christ's farewell to His disciples, John 13.1–17.26.
to leave this world. 'Is mind purely spiritual
as Christians believe? Or has it a material basis in the brain?

Our moral sense is based on our affection! Love
of divinity – effect of organization. Social behaviour
needed in some species to survive. Love must come
from the organic, not any spiritual feature of our being.'

His feet hurt. Five baby cockroaches, hatched below
the boards of Great Marlborough Street kitchen,
gather like amber soot in a crack of skirting
ready to whisk inside the cistern when he moves.

In a while you shall not see me. A little while more and you shall John 16.16.
again. 'Must demonstrate the basis of all things beautiful,
in sentiment of animated creatures, is the social
instinct.' *I shall not leave you comfortless.* 'But men John 14.18.

have personified deity so completely! Argument
for materialism: that cold water, thrown on the head,
produces a frame of mind very similar to feelings
considered spiritual. If, as I hold, thought and perception rise

from physical action on the brain, that renders
instincts of the animals much less wonderful:
less of a surprise.' He knows (how could he not,
having read Divinity?) all this will be attacked as heresy.

John 18.1. *They went out over the brook called Cedron*
where a garden was. And Judas knew the spot.
'To avoid showing how far I believe in the material,
say only hereditary talent comes about because

child's brain resembles parent stock. Must work
in solitude, build evidence in silence. Cannot risk argument
till certain of the ground.' He can feel his doubt. It flows
at the rate of lava, ten hours for every inch. He lays no store

by soul-searching or prayer. Creation, Fall of Man, Eternal Life:
they're beating on his tenderness like waves on a coral reef.
A purposeful, wise, *beneficent* divinity? That First Cause
which gave rise to the radiant stage of outer space,

gazelle dance of heavenly bodies round the sun, beginnings
of sentient life? He wants, so much, to believe as she desires.
(The night is squashing him like magma.) But he can't buy
the Old Testament's revenge-filled deity;

and Christ's message, in the New, fulfils its prophecies.
John 14.16–17. *I'll send my Comforter, the Spirit of the Truth –*
but where's the proof? Couldn't God, if He meant us to believe
all this, have given a more credible foundation?

HE PITCHES A DEAD DOG OUT OF THE GARDEN

London and Maer Hall, November 1838 to January 1839.

Charles.

'Like a child
  that has something it loves beyond measure,
I long to dwell on the words –
  my own dear Emma.
My chief fear is, that you will find,

after living all your life with parties
  as only Maer can boast, our quiet evenings dull.
You must bear in mind
  all men are brutes. And I take the line
of being a solitary brute. You must listen

with suspicion
  to my arguments for a retired place as our home.
I am so deeply selfish that I feel
  to have you to myself, alone,
is having you the so much more completely.'

*

Emma.

'You will consider me a specimen
of the genus I don't know what –
Simia, I believe.

When we move in,
you will be forming theories
about me all the time.'

*

Charles.

'I was thinking how on earth it came that I,
that am fond of talking
and hardly ever out of spirits,

should so entirely rest
my notions of happiness
on quiet. The explanation, I believe,

is very simple. During the voyage
my whole pleasure was derived
from what passed in my own mind

admiring by myself extraordinary views
while travelling wild desert
and glorious forest. Excuse

this much egotism! I give it to you
because you will soon teach me
there's greater happiness

than building theories
and accumulating facts
in silence and solitude.'

*

Emma.

'If I am cross or out of temper
you will only say,
"What does that prove?"

Which will be a very grand
and philosophical way
of considering the matter.'

*

Charles.

'. . . until I am a part
of you
my own dear Emma . . .'

*

'It's well I'm coming to look after you
my poor old man. You're evidently on the verge
of insanity, wandering streets
smothered in "To Let" signs. Emma.

We'll have to advertise! Lost, in the vicinity
of Bloomsbury, a tall thin gentleman,
quite harmless. Whoever brings him back
will be rewarded, handsomely.'

*

'I have found a house I think will do Charles.
but the drawing-room

has yellow curtains with *blue*
furniture and door!

All the colours of the macaw
in hideous discord.'

*

'It is my most earnest wish Charles.
that I may make
myself worthy of you, dearest Emma.'

*

The dead dog lay
in the garden among black trees in smoky fog.

If you touched a branch your fingers smeared
with soot. But this was ordinary –

when you'd been out in a London street
two hours, the glory of your laundry

and clear starcher disappeared
in a myriad of *flocculi*

called blacks. Soot stuck to ladies' pleats
and gentlemen's collars equally.

*

Charles.

'Is it not *our* house? What is there, from me,
the geologist, to the black

sparrows in the garden,
that is not your property?'

*

Charles.

'My study so still, so peaceful
after Gt Marlborough Street.
Covington helped me move in.

Natural history specimens – two vans!
Dozens of drawers of shells we took by hand.
The front attic, door to window-sill,

is filled. I call it the Museum.
I wish I could make the drawing-room
as comfortable as my studio

but I dare say a fire, a piano
and a little disorder will do!
If one is quiet in London

there's nothing like it. You will see
there is a grandeur about the smoke, the fogs
and soot, the dull distant throb of cabs

like remote sea.' He has funny ideas about grandeur.
'I hope, with your help, gradually
to grow to be less of a brute.'

*

'Married, St Peter's Church, today
at Maer. Weather not chill, really.

Emma, 29 January 1839.

You might even say kind. Very quiet.
In London, our first Thursday,

we went slopping through melted snow
to Broadwoods. I tried Mozart on a piano –

we asked if it could be delivered to our house.
On Saturday we ventured out again and saw the van.

Charles shouted, *Is that for us?*
We learned to our great satisfaction that it was.

I have given him a largish dose
of music every evening.'

*

At night, a single rattling cab
    seems to her to last for ever.
They go together to
    Handel's *Messiah*, Bellini's
La Sonnambula; the Zoo.

CONFINEMENT

I

SYMPTOMS

January 1839. The British East India Company
captures Aden. In March 'OK', from *orl korrect*,
appears first time in the *Boston Evening Globe.*
Michael Faraday clarifies the nature of electricity.
In April, she writes 'Pregnant'. A telegraph line
starts work beside Great Western Railway, from Paddington
to West Drayton. In June, Louis Daguerre
receives full patent for a camera. The photograph:
a system, one understands, for writing with the sun.

July. British forces take the gateway to Kabul.
Five thousand British troops escort a puppet Shah
to the throne of Ghazni, famous for minarets
in the shape of stars. The Pashtun tribesmen don't like him.
August 1839. We're in the First Anglo-Afghan War: it's going to limp on
for years. People who know say no outside power
can keep the kingdom of Afghanistan impregnable
for ever. In Upper Gower Street she writes,
'Halfway now I think, from the symptoms.'

II

SHE WRITES HIM A NOTE ABOUT SALVATION

'When I talk to you face to face I cannot say
exactly what I wish.' Her back aches all the time;
she never goes out. His friend's wife has died
in childbirth. 'You say you are uncertain
about Christian Revelation but your opinion
is still not formed.' He's told her his discoveries:

While pregnant, Emma wrote a letter to Charles (though they were living together), worried that if he did not believe, he would not be saved; so if she died she would never see him again.

she'd love him to be right in everything. She's very afraid
he's not. 'Faith is beyond our comprehension,
not provable in the scientific way you like.
I believe you sincerely wish to learn the truth.
But there are dangers in giving up Revelation
and Christ's offer of eternal life. And in the sin –

Darwin meanwhile was publishing his *Journal of Researches*, later known as *Voyage of the Beagle*.

I know you will have patience with your own
dear wife – of ingratitude for His suffering,
casting off what has been done. For you,
for everyone. I do not wish an answer.
It is satisfaction for me just to write. My fear
is for the afterlife. I cannot say how happy

you make me in this one, nor how dearly I love you.
I thank you for all the affection, which makes
my happiness more and more each day.
But everything that concerns you concerns me.
I should be most unhappy if I thought
we would not belong to each other for eternity.'

III

HE LEAVES A MESSAGE ON THE EDGE

Darwin left Emma's letter, with his message on it, for her to find after his death in 1882.

He kept her note all his life. He must have said
something then, but he wrote to her too
on the outer fold. (No one knows when.
He was maybe quite old. He wasn't blind
to where his thought led, what she thought
she'd lose.) 'When I am dead, know
I have kissed and cried over this many times.'

IV

HOG'S LARD

Their first child, William, was born 27 December 1839.

She's walking a dark shoreline, trusting
the Saviour's suffering and comfort:
but it's hard. Behind the accoucheur,
a midwife with towels, hot water, lard.

From a book by a contemporary obstetrician, James Blundell, 1840.

A newly-married woman dreads examination.
Therefore sit by the bed and talk of other things.
Gateways of the flesh like stubborn gods.
Colours of a journey: smoking dung.
Get the nurse to ask how baby lies.

This makes her anxious about it.
She's burning. Words form
on her lips like miraculous fish
bearing a gold ring, and rush away again.
When a pang comes, put your hand

on the sacrum to relieve pain.
This mystery of love. Darkness
across the world on stretchy wings.
Next time there is a wave of anguish
slip two fingers into the vagina.

She tries to feel the pain as kinder
but it's a battering-ram, a guillotine inside.
Ascertain the passages are open, the pubis arch
natural. Flame in her eye-sockets; a maroon map
of South America. *For us and all mankind* . . .

An axe, a knife – *feel for the os uteri* –
and something pulling away. She sees the midwife
bind cloth round something tiny. Behind the glass
night pleats an indigo-and-black accordion.
She's going to go through this ten times:

pregnant, in labour or recovering, the whole
next sixteen years. After the fifth she'll write,
'I wonder if I might have the luck
to escape another soon.' But no.

V

RAW LEMON

Waiting, like a hermit on a pole
forty nights in bare
desert. The cries. *Thock thock*
like beating a dog.

This black script of pain.
His own tongue
tasting a devil's cup
of bitter lemon.

'What an awful affair
confinement is!
It knocked me up
nearly as much as Emma.'

A NATURAL HISTORY OF BABIES

'Things to know about babies.'
A pink fist. Fontanelles.
'My little animalcule of a son . . .'

*

'. . . occurred last Friday week.
It is a little prince! . . .'

*

'Had not smallest conception
there was so much in a five-month baby.'

*

'You will conclude I have a fine degree
of paternal fervour! He is a prodigy
of beauty and intellect – so charming
I cannot pretend to any modesty.'

*

'I at once commenced
to make notes on the expressions
he exhibited, looking for the earliest
signs of each emotion

to see the emergence
of human nature: how our ancestors
became what we are. I felt convinced,
even at this early period,

Darwin observed and made notes on all his babies and toddlers, especially William the first and Annie the second.

Their ten children were Willie, born 1839; Annie, born 1841 (died aged ten); Mary, born 1842 (died aged three weeks); Etty, born 1843; George, born 1845; Bessie, born 1847; Francis, born 1848; Leonard, born 1850; Horace, born 1851; Charles Waring, born 1856 (died aged one and a half).

that the most complex
and fine shades
of expression must all have
a gradual and a natural origin.'

*

'Do babies startle – that is, make
    useless muscle movements
very early? Do they frown
    when they first see? Or shrink
when you place a thing in front of them
    before experience
has taught them about danger?'

*

He will carry on observing with all ten.
Sixteen years of playing, smiling, wondering
at stirring tissue: at the human

suddenly awake like painted bison, bearded
and palaeolithic in the bowels of a cave,
shaking their shaggy selves off a streaming wall,

dodging stalactites, tossing dreadlocks,
longhuddling towards the light. A *whang*
of feathered forelegs over rock.

Human babies, one after the other:
all, in movement and expression, so
like Jenny, the orang-utang.

*

'He sat on my knee
for upward of a quarter of an hour . . .

A smile,
probably of mental origin . . .'

*

'His reflexes, immediately perfect.
Voluntary actions though, imperfect.

At thirty-two days he perceived
his mother's bosom, three
or four inches away. As you could see

from the protrusion of his lips
and his eyes being fixed . . .'

*

'. . . anxious to observe
accurately

the expression
of a crying child

but sympathy with his grief
spoiled all my observation.'

ON THE DISTRIBUTION OF ERRATIC BOULDERS

I

FATHER SAYS I MAY OFTEN TAKE CALOMEL

Calomel, mercurous chloride, is toxic but was often used both as a laxative and 'disinfectant'.

Their second child, Annie, was born in March 1841.

Darwin and his family spent summer holidays at Maer. Staying there in 1841, Darwin had the first severe bout of the illness he suffered for the rest of his life. In summer 1842 he wrote there a pencil sketch of his secret theory: what became natural selection and its part in evolution.

He's been ill. Now he's writing in pencil, at dusk. Doughy scent
of roses from the flower garden at Maer.
He hears his baby daughter, laughing. From now on
being ill will rule his life. The word 'Dinosaur' is being coined
for Iguanadon, a fossil from remote geologic past.
Pashtun tribesmen have killed that Afghan Shah;
the British have fallen back to the Khyber Pass. Next year
they'll be massacred there entirely. Cretans have rebelled
against Ottoman rule and been repressed. Five Great Powers
guarantee Ottoman sovereignty over Crete; they've recognized
the Sultan's right to close the Bosphorus and Dardanelles
to foreign warships. He'll put away *Descent*
with Modification. Gather evidence, stay silent,
not hurt Emma. Let this sketch think about itself
in darkness like a prophet in a cave. He'll do geology.
On the Distribution of Erratic Boulders. The Structure
of Coral Reefs. 'When finished with other projects
I'll write a book about Varieties & Species.'

II

SHE THINKS THE HAIRS UNDER HIS ARM GROW LIKE A CRESCENT MOON

He lies with one hand on her belly, where the next
child's grown. She'd like to get up and tell the kitchen
about rabbit for tonight, but he is still inside her.
('Above any woman,' they will all say afterwards,
'she comforted.') He leads with his chin when he sleeps.
Orange freckles on his upper arm like flecks
in a foxglove bell. She knows their clustering by heart.
'He seems to be putting God further and further off.'
This is what it is, to love – to lie, not moving,
staring at city light half-hidden by a curtain.
Every morning he vomits in the basin.
His illness lives with them like another child.
This sheet is a rising tide of snow above her eye.
He's heavily asleep. Black sparrows chitter outside.

In summer 1842 Emma was pregnant with their third child, Mary.

DOWNE

I

THE EXTREME VERGE OF THE WORLD

In July 1842 they went to view the house that became their new home: Down House outside the village of Downe, in Kent.

They're dreaming of a garden like the ones they knew
as children. They've searched the railway routes
so he can talk science in London and come back home
for dinner. They've lost a house in Woking –

now it's Kent. A gloomy day. Bolts of blue
from a chilly north-east wind. Sixteen miles –
two hours by train. Fat hedgerows, skeined with paper trails
of wild white clematis, and ancient wooded hills.

Step out. It feels remote. An old flint church:
St Mary's, Downe. A yew, a walnut tree with bark
like silver hair. Villagers smile from open doors.
The butcher, baker, post office. The villa they've come to see.

'Ugly,' she says. 'A desolate air.' The garden, though,
makes up for it. Old trees – purple magnolia, a quince,
a medlar, Spanish chestnut. A goodish hay-meadow.
In September they'll move in. A child will be born,

Mary Darwin was born 23 September 1842, died 16 October and was buried in Downe churchyard.

and buried in the family plot he'll pick at the west door
of this flint church. Through briar rose haws, twisting petioles
of clematis will scribble these hedges like the pencil
of a ferocious toddler with glowing, ochre-coloured wire.

II

A SACRED FEELING ABOUT ORCHIDS

All the flowers that grew at Down were beautiful; and different from all other flowers.

Gwen Raverat, *Period Piece*, 1952

Children butt like young bulls in his study. He reads to them
about Ohio – life would be cheaper there! – and they upturn
his sofa, play 'emigrating to the prairies'. He walks through
the green baize door like no other gentleman, to skeletonize
fancy pigeons in the kitchen. Children take turns, even Emma –
Mammy, he calls her now – on the Staircase Slide.

Down House, 1842–70.

He takes the cook's hand at whist, so she can get on
with dinner, and walks alone in woods at sunrise:
slow, each step without a sound, a foot-in-air wait
before the next, as in the forests of Brazil.
One day he sees a polecat. He watches a vixen
play with her cubs, only a few feet distant.

Sometimes he takes a child along. They'll all have memories.
'Misty red sunrise.' 'The glory of being with him
in the woods.' 'I fancy he used to conceal from me
the rare birds he observed, goldfinch, siskin,
because he saw my agony at not seeing them.'
'He said he had a kind of sacred feeling about orchids

Several of Darwin's children left written memoirs of him.

and taught us to have it too. On our picnic bank, among
    the juniper, we found the fly, twyblade and musk
varieties.' 'When winter came, puddles froze
    to a shining white. A delightful crackling sound
when trodden. Mysterious, because the frost
    had drunk them dry in roofing them with ice.'

'In spring, lambs staggering, half-fledged in the cold
    fields among the turnips.' 'On May Day
village children came from house to house, singing
    with cherry boughs, collecting pennies for the pole.'
'In summer the lawn burnt brown. Rattle of the fly-wheel
    of the well. The scented lime trees, humming with bees –

and my father lying under them on grass. Children playing
    with a kitten. My mother in lilac muslin
wondering why the blackcaps did not sing here
    the song they sang when she was a girl, at Maer.'
'At midsummer, we'd wake to hear the mowers whetting scythes.
    The field had been a great and sacred sea

we might not enter. Tall grass, white with daisies,
    pink with sorrel. Now we could follow them in,
watch grasses fall and a track grow beneath their feet.
    Beyond the swathes a sea-green stack rose like a candle
in a corner of the field. The cart enchantingly polished
    inside, and filled with seed.'

III

THE CONFESSION

'At last gleams of light have come.
  Contrary to the opinion I started with
  I am almost convinced
that species are not (it is like confessing
to a murder) immutable. I think I have found
  (here's presumption!) the simple way
  by which species become
adapted to new ends.'

Letter to the botanist J. D. Hooker, 11 January 1844.

IV

THE POND SPIRIT

'In winter, invisible owls called
  from one moonlit tree to another.
When we skated, a wicked groaning squeak

ran round the solitary pond
  when it settled down, unwillingly,
to bear us on its surface.

It had a threat in it, reminding us
  we were helpless. The pond spirit
was our master and held our lives in its grip.'

V

MORE FUNNY IDEAS ABOUT GRANDEUR

Down House, 1844.

'To Emma, in case of my sudden death.
I have just finished this sketch
of my species theory. If true, as I believe,
it will be a considerable step
in science. My most solemn last request
is that you devote 400 pounds
to its publication.'

'There is grandeur, if you look
at every organic being
as the lineal successor of some other form,
now buried under thousands of feet of rock.
Or else as a co-descendant, with that buried form,
from some other inhabitant of this world
more ancient still, now lost.

Out of famine, death and struggle for existence,
comes the most exalted end
we're capable of conceiving: creation
of the higher animals!
Our first impulse is to disbelieve –
how could any secondary law
produce organic beings, infinitely numerous,

characterized by most exquisite
workmanship and adaptation?
Easier to say, a Creator designed each.
But there is a simple grandeur in this view –
that life, with its power to grow, to reach, feel,
reproduce, diverge, was breathed
into matter in a few forms first

and maybe only one. To say that while this planet
has gone cycling on
according to fixed laws of gravity,
from so simple an origin, through selection
of infinitesimal varieties, endless forms
most beautiful and wonderful
have been, and are being, evolved.'

EPIPHANY IN LEICESTER PUBLIC LIBRARY

In 1845 Darwin published a revised edition of his book about the voyage and called it *Journal of the Voyage of the Beagle*. Alfred Russel Wallace read it in the Leicester Public Library.

Someone you've never heard of. Nor has anyone else.
Plump, working-class, dark glossy curls
and standing by the clock tower in Leicester.
A land-surveyor: Welsh, twenty-one and just sacked
(times are hard) by his brother. Now he's walking down
High Street, looking for the public library, Guild Hall.

He's got a job at the Collegiate School. He loves
outdoors, he's tough, but now he can afford
to study, too. An arch of small red bricks. Above,
the black and white East Wing; beneath, the Borough's
cells for its new Police. Inside, the blissful bookshelves,
balconies and polished floor. His carrel is tropical

mahogany, a ruby dream of charcoal.
He reads Malthus. Then *Journal of the Voyage
of the Beagle*. 'An inspiration! My determination
to hunt butterflies and beetles in the tropics
dated from that book.' Hard bulbs of want explode
under his heart. To understand variety! Unravel,

if he can, the mystery of evolution; travel
to the tropics and simply – well – collect.
In the brown-black gloam of closing-time
he meets his future colleague, a published
entomologist. 'I had no idea! So many thousand
different beetles within ten miles of home!'

In the Library Wallace also met the entomologist with whom, four years later, he made his first collecting expedition, self-financed, to Brazil.

THE SEA WILL DO US ALL GOOD

'Annie listless.' They take her to Ramsgate
          to try what sea water can do. On the beach
he picks up shells. He is still a collector. Emma
          watches a bathing-woman in baggy blue
coax Annie to the caravan-machine
          drawn by two horses out to sea. She thinks through
in her head a Beethoven sonata and cadenza.

In 1846, Darwin published *Geological Observations on South America*.
In autumn 1850 his ten-year-old daughter Annie was unwell. Charles and Emma took her to Ramsgate.

Every day behind a stripy awning,
          Blue Woman lowers Annie into sea.
But Annie catches cold. Then influenza.
          He takes her, with sister Etty for company,
to Malvern. Emma, seven months pregnant, stays behind.
          'If the girls take letters to Malvern post office
by six, I'll receive them at our garden gate by noon.'

In March 1851 Darwin took Annie and her seven-year-old sister Etty to Malvern for a month. He settled them with the children's nurse in a water-cure establishment at the centre of town and arranged for the children's governess, Catherine Thorley, to join them.

*

She stands in the flower garden. A wind like chain mail
sweeps the grass.

*

'Mamma, I have six ladybirds in a box.
I feed them milk and sugar.'

Letter from Etty, 1851.

*

'Let Mr Darwin come back at once to Malvern.
Annie very ill, with a smart, bilious, gastric fever.'

The governess, Catherine Thorley.

*

Charles.

'Annie a fearful mess. Vomit, diarrhoea.
    We keep her sweet with chloride of lime.
We sponged her today with vinegar and water
    to excellent effect. I will write to you every hour.
It is a relief to me. Whilst writing I can cry
    very tranquilly.'

*

Good Friday. Three retching fits. Emerald fluid.

Charles.

'It seems an exaggerated form of my own illness.
She inherits, I fear, my own wretched digestion.'

Emma asked her brother's wife Fanny (who now bore the same name, Fanny Wedgwood, as her own dead sister) to go to Malvern to be with Charles. Fanny's maid took Etty back to Down.

Saturday. 'Your cousin has come. Dr Gully still has hope . . .
Oh my dear be thankful. Annie has rallied. Passed a good
night. Danger much less imminent.'

*

Emma.

'I received your cable by electric
    telegraph. I was in the garden, alone,
        looking at my poor darling's little patch
    of flowers. I hardly dare think of such happiness.
I hope you will sleep tonight, my own.'

*

Emma to Fanny Wedgwood.

'I feel most anxious about Charles, dear cousin,
but your being with him is such a comfort.

By oneself, one's thoughts lose all control.
The worst, for me, is waiting for the post.'

*

Easter Sunday. Downe church altar gay
with apple blossom. A day of loose
flowers and hope. There is One who holds

the petals' falling in His hands. She stays home –
final stage of pregnancy – to pray
while the six other children are at church.

*

He cannot sit quiet. He has to pace the room
and write to her. 'The doctor says Charles.
there still is hope. But you would not recognize
her poor sharp hard pinched face.'

*

Monday. Red, brightly mottled things
swarm over and through his eyelids.
'The alternatives, hope and no hope, Charles.
sicken the soul. A mustard poultice
on her stomach smarted her a good deal
but when we sponged her down
delicious to see how it soothed!

I never saw anything so pathetic as her patience.
She has just said "Papa" quite distinctly.
She does not suffer, thank God.
The note from you
made me cry much, but I must not give way.
It is, from hour to hour, a struggle between life
and death. God only knows the issue.'

*

Fanny Wedgwood.

Tuesday. 'I grieve to tell you, dearest Emma –
Charles cannot write – a worse report

this evening. The end seems near. We are thankful
for the mercy given us of there being, in your sweet

patient darling, not the least appearance
of suffering. Twice in her delirium

I heard her trying to sing – so I think the wandering
could not have been distressing.'

*

Wednesday morning. The sky a livid iron-grey

Fanny Wedgwood.

and overcast. 'At twelve o'clock came a peal
of thunder and we heard her breathe her last.'

*

Emma.

Thursday. 'Till four o'clock, not having heard,
I sometimes had a hope. But when I went to bed
I felt as if it all had happened long ago.

Among the prayers and tears, my only thought
of consolation is to have you safe at home
and weep together. I am so full of fears

about you, dear Charles. They are not reasonable
fears, but my powers of hoping seem all gone.
I can't bear to think of you alone.'

*

Friday. 'Our dear had a very short life Charles.
but I trust happy. She expired without a sigh
and God only knows what more miseries might,
with her constitution, have lain in store.

Do what you can to bear up.' An ocean. An abyss.
He hears a bell begin to toll. Myth
lets you say something and not say it, too.
He can't stay for the funeral, can't pray for Annie's future bliss.

'Remember how kind you always were to her.'
Their next is due in three weeks. 'I long to be with you
and under your protection; for then I feel safe.
I am in bed, not very well – my own poor, dear, dear wife.'

CHAPTER FIVE

THE COAT OF FUR

1851–1882

THE OSTRICH

I

THE DEVIL'S CHAPLAIN

Reticence descends on the house
like an ostrich on its nest: a belljar of black feathers.
Etty, missing her sister, terrified of all
the not-talking. 'I am afraid, Mama, of going to hell.'

Down House, 1851.

O tumbling humans and their languages! O burin,
that chisel of tempered steel used for engraving,
keen as a unicorn – or a mind
pursuing argument and proof. 'Do you think

you shall come to heaven with me Mama?' 'I hope so, yes.
And we shall have Annie too.' The red ants battle black.
Rainwind lashes trees in the garden and the leaves toss,
they bash the rain back. 'Nature is prodigal of the forms

of life. The fit will be preserved, the weak
exterminated utterly – as myriads have been before:
battle within battle, ever recurring.'
Annie was, if you have to say these things, his favourite.

On the Origin of Species, Chapter 4.

He sees a parade of huge black dinosaurs with smoky breath.
'Nature is prodigal of time. She scrutinizes every muscle,
vessel, nerve. Every habit, instinct, shade
of constitution. There will be no caprice, no favouring.'

She's asked him not to change his views
for fear of giving her pain. 'Annie,
with her loving ways, seemed formed to live a life
of happiness.' He's put Christian faith behind.

On Sundays he walks the family to church
and leaves them at the door. 'What a book
a devil's chaplain might write
on nature's blundering works!'

She knows he will always need proof.
He knows that she, his Comforter, needs Comfort too.
'So profound is our ignorance, and so high
our presumption, that we marvel

when we hear of any being going extinct!
We do not see the cause.
So we invoke cataclysm – a Flood
to desolate the world – or invent laws

to explain how forms of life endure.'
He stands outside St Mary's door, chatting
to the village constable, then heads into the lanes
to look for birds. 'The universe we observe,

if properly understood, has all the properties
we should expect if there is no purpose, no design,
no evil and no good. Nothing but blind, pitiless
indifference.' He does believe in a Divine Creator still

but not hers, not wise and kind. A ruthless shadowy thing
eternally going in for cruelty, elimination, waste.
'How Annie ran downstairs with a pinch of stolen
snuff for me, her whole form radiant with the pleasure

of giving pleasure! Oh that she could know
how deeply we shall ever love her joyous face!'
The harmony of nature comes direct
from what he's witnessed. 'Each form eternally destroyed

while others take its place.' There's violence
under the bright surface all the time. 'The pain
will never fade. We have lost our treasure,
joy of the household, solace of our old age.'

II

SUBMISSION TO THE WILL OF HEAVEN

Death, for the Christian, is bound up with sin.
    The connection is like a medical condition, or an engine
thudding along moon-splashed channels of the brain.

'I feel grateful to God that our darling was apparently   Down House, 1851.
    spared suffering. I hope I shall be able to attain
submission to the will of Heaven.' She packs a small

memento box, Annie's writing case. She seals it
    and hardly speaks of Annie again. When she does,
the sense of loss erupts, bald as a vulture, unhealed.

III

CHLOROFORM

1852.

Will the Queen try chloroform, for her eighth child?
No one then will say that stopping this pain is wrong.
But playing a Bourrée with a jar of worms on the piano lid
(so Charles will know if they can hear) she hopes the child-bearing
may end. Leonard, last year, was the first with chloroform.

Leonard was born in 1850; Annie died in March 1851; Horace was born three weeks afterwards.

'I thought,' Charles told his friends, 'I was only soothing pain –
but Emma remembered nothing till she heard the child was born.
Is that not grand? The greatest, most blessed of discoveries.'
Again with Horace, three weeks after Annie's death.
She's had two miscarriages since. Surely seven children is
enough.

ENCOUNTER IN THE BACKROOM OF THE INSECT COLLECTION

He's back, this chubby Welshman, from a shipwreck
in Brazil, and living on insurance from his specimens
lost at sea. He's thirty, poor and driven, negligent of health
to a point you might call suicidal. Yellow fever, cholera,
who cares? These eighteen months in town he's written
six scientific papers ('Monkeys of the Amazon' for instance)
and two books. But here's the real high: saying hello,
fleetingly, to his alibi self. Waistcoats. Grey cloth.
A masculine handshake over shiny wings and beetle pins.
Behind these darkpool eyes, fourteen years older than his own,
these broad shoulders and black sideburns, is his idol.

Alfred Russel Wallace first met Darwin at the Natural History Museum in 1853.
The two men corresponded while Wallace was away. Darwin asked Wallace to send him skins of Malaysian poultry. A mutually supportive friendship continued until Darwin's death.

He knows now what *he* is good at, what he loves:
identifying, in jungle, each butterfly or bird.
He adores each complex form – as this man does.
Over the years, this author's books have spurred
him on. He worships Darwin's articles, editing, observing;
the questions and connections; the ideas.
Now he's off to the Malay peninsula. He sees a rope
of shining islands on a red horizon. He'll finance
himself by selling to collectors rare beetles, birdskins,
mammal skeletons. Probing the world's
magna mysteria. Prospecting Nature's gold.

I NEVER SAW A MORE STRIKING COINCIDENCE

I

SURVIVAL OF THE FITTEST

From September 1854 I devoted my whole time to arranging my huge pile of notes, to observing and to experimenting in relation to the transmutation of species.

Darwin, *Autobiography*

In 1853 Darwin was publicly recognized as a scientist when the Royal Society gave him a Gold Medal, both for his geology publications from the *Beagle* voyage and for his publications on barnacles (Cirripedia), research which had taken him seven years and made him a world authority on the subject.

'I've sent ten thousand barnacles out of the house
and am sorting species notes. I am unusually well
but excitement and fatigue bring on dreadful flatulence.'
He doesn't say 'fart'. Maybe he doesn't know the word.
'Breeding domestic animals, you get rid of sickly offspring.'

His seven years' research on Cirripedia has proved
sexual selection superior, in throwing off disease,
to propagation by hermaphrodite. With Etty, he's bred
and dissected a thousand fancy pigeons to demonstrate
they're all descended from the same rock dove.

Darwin bred many different kinds of pigeon, belonged to several pigeon clubs in London and spent hours talking to pigeon breeders.

'Pouters', 'Tipplers', and 'Fan-Toes'. White down
on pink claws like pleats of a ballerina
curtsying the floor. 'Mortal illness in man due,
no doubt, to hereditary tendencies towards disease
which clears away the weak.'

Was it because of him that Annie died?
'My dread is hereditary ill-health.
Are marriages between first cousins doomed
to deformity and illness? Effects
of inbreeding – only the fittest survive?'

II

JOURNEY UP THE SADONG RIVER

From Wallace's accounts of a trip to north-west Borneo in 1855, on which he became the first naturalist to see one of the Great Apes in its natural habitat.

'I intended to devote the dry season to exploring
the interior, but a wound in my foot left me unable to walk,
even leave my room for three months, till the rains began.
Abundance of jasper, pure white pebbles and quartz

on the riverbed. The banks overgrown
with durian trees whose spiny fruit, size of a melon,
deserves to be ranked as king of fruits. White rock
and twisted limestone cliffs; the ground a black morass

of mud. Twenty miles up, a stream enters: the Simunjon.
Here, on a lonely mountain, the great orang-utang, or Mias,
is abundant. It roams this vast unbroken forest
as easily as the Indian in the prairie, the Arab in the desert.

It is a singular, most interesting sight, to watch a Mias
make his way leisurely through forest, semi-erect
along the branches, seeming at once to resemble and to mock
the human form divine. So close are they to us

in structure, so different in points of their external form.
But animals most isolated in existing nature have been shown
to be just the most recent of a series
of allied species which lived before upon the earth, and died.

The Mias swings forward by forming a bridge between the trees.
He pulls a handful of twigs from the next tree, mingles them
with the one he is on, seizes a branch with his long arm –
and is at once on the opposite side.

He never jumps or hurries but moves as quick as a man
beneath can run. They seem not much alarmed at man,
staring down several minutes then, moving slowly away.
After seeing one, I have gone a mile or more to fetch my gun

and found the animal on return within a hundred yards.
Females have but one young, which clings to its mother's hair
and gets in her way so little that twice I was not aware
of the babe until both fell together.' He looked after one

baby for three months, until it died. 'When pursued, they make
for the nearest lofty tree and throw branches down at you
to terrify their attacker. One female kept a continuous shower
of durians like cannon fire. We could see her

breaking them off, hurling them with rage, uttering
loud pumping snorts and evidently intending mischief.
They eat only fruit but have enormous teeth –
almost beyond belief, how they tear the outer skin

of a durian, so thick, so tough, so full of conical spines.
They don't attack other animals and few – a crocodile, they say,
but I have never seen it – will attack them. When forced to defend
themselves, they use arms and legs. They do not bite:

so why the massive teeth? But many animals have appendages
which serve no physical purpose. To explain this
we must find a principle more recondite
than individual need. Naturalists are too apt to *imagine*,

when they cannot *discover*, a use for everything
in nature. When badly wounded, a Mias begins
to make a nest. If they finish it they never fall.
I lost two that way, both dying on their nest.

Their tenacity of life is very great – six to a dozen
bullets are required to kill them. But once seen
there's no danger they will get away.
I managed to shoot thirteen.'

III

SALTING THE SEEDS

Down House, 1855–56. Darwin experimented to see if seeds survived immersion in salt water; wishing to show how plants might have reached the Galapagos and adapted differently on each island.

'Comparing seeds. Trying experiments
in salting them to see if they'd survive
floating across an ocean.'
To, for instance, the Galapagos.

In spring 1856 Darwin confessed to the geologist Charles Lyell his secret views on species and transmutation. Lyell urged him to publish an essay to establish his priority to these ideas. In June Darwin reluctantly began to do so, worried that it would be 'very imperfect'.

'Have begun, at last, my species book. Shall call it
Natural Selection.' His secret step in argument.
Twenty years of evidence. Orchids, barnacles
and pigeons. The heart dances in its cave.

He meets the holes of his eyes in darkling glass
against the winter garden. No one awake.
Slow embers in the grate. The dog, a warm
white ammonite, curled

in her basket by his feet. Dawn fog dissolves
among the medlars into a wraith
you see, then lose, in the shape
of a running girl.

IV

PAINTING THE BEES

The questions buzz at him like birds. They cling
  like burrs, delight him like the children, paw like dogs.
They scratch, torment and swarm; they pollinate
like wasps. It's got to be vast – proof, evidence,
minutiae. Orchids, fertilizing in the greenhouse.
  Birdskins from India, horse-markings of Norway, finch
beaks from Galapagos, a parcel of flora from Kew.

How contain all this? Vomit. Panic. Vomit. Nerves
  in his neck. That wagtail on the lawn –
what muscles make it flick like that; what purpose
does it serve? Flatulence; bad headache;
halfway through. He steps out to his thinking path,
  the Sandwalk. Remembering the trail around the lake
at Maer, they have designed a circuit round a copse.

Walking each question through the undergrowth
  with his terrier, he leaves a pebble at the start
of every lap. Into the Dark Side (so the children call it
and the little ones are scared), of ivy, tall trees, bushes,
lords and ladies, evergreens. Out
  past the sandpit to the Light Side's open view
of cloudshadow in Great Pucklands Meadow. Sun.

Down House, 1857. Darwin much enjoyed involving the children in his experiments, which were often quite wild: 'Many untenable theories occurred to him,' says Francis Darwin in his memoir, but 'fortunately' he was as quick to criticize and condemn what did not work as to dream up new possibilities.

He loves that the children play here. A bugle and boy-laughter –
that's Frank and Georgy in Crimea. He's drilled them with
toy rifles,
taught them parts of a gun. Since *Beagle*, he hasn't used one.
('Shooting is cruel.') They're warming their campfire
milk. 'Whatever my father did with us', they will say after,
'had over it a glamour of delight.' His Fool's Experiments!
'I shan't be easy till I've tried . . .' – as if some outside force

were at him with a truncheon. He sets the girls to search
for wormcasts. 'Damp evenings are best.'
Horace finds him snake and lizard eggs, Frank plays bassoon
to worms (are they really deaf?) and even flowers
to see how they like vibration. He strings all seven children over
long grass and scabious in a chain, to paint
and track the bumblebees who pollinate red clover.

V

A BIRTHDAY ON THE ISLAND OF TERNATE

Ambon, *Aru*, *Banda*, *Halmahera*, *Morotai*, *Bacan* . . .
(I'm trying to remember Spice Islands where Wallace went
for his *Malay Archipelago*.) On Bacan he found a prize –
no, two. Both beautiful. Wallace's Golden Bird-Wing Butterfly
and Wallace's Standard-Wing Bird of Paradise.

'At dawn on 8 January I arrived at the island of Ternate,
lying under the equator.' His birthday, as it happens;
his thirty-fifth. 'One of a row of conical volcanic islands.'
Empire of the clove. A sultanate.
'The town is concealed from view

till you enter between two islands and see it stretched
along the shore at the base of a huge mountain
furrowed with deep gullies, covered in groves of fruit:
banana, mango, lime; papaya, cassava, durian.
From the summit issue wreaths of smoke. It looks calm,

but beneath are hidden fires, which occasionally burst forth
in lava-streams and make their existence known by earthquakes
which devastate the town.' The whole place glisters with gold
from centuries of trade. Jewels, silver, the finest work
of India and of Europe, brought here in exchange for cloves.

The riches he anticipates are different.
'I have been much gratified by a letter from Darwin!
He agrees with *almost every word* of my last paper!
He is now preparing his great work on Species and Varieties,
for which he has been collecting material twenty years.

In January 1858, Wallace was in the North Molucca Islands: 'The Spice Islands', now part of Indonesia.

Asked afterwards why it was himself and Darwin who discovered the role of natural selection in evolution, Wallace said they were both avid beetle-hunters early on; both were fascinated by variety and loved collecting; both observed variety in action in the place of the greatest variety, the tropics; and both read Malthus at a key point in their thinking.

Another vital factor was that they both saw variety in action on a group of islands.

He may save me the trouble of writing more
on my hypothesis by proving there is no difference
between the origin of species and varieties.
Or he may give me trouble by arriving at another conclusion.
At least his facts will be given me, to work upon.'

VI

THE HUMAN FORM DIVINE

Down House, February 1858. Their tenth child, Charles Waring, was born in December 1856.

He walks up and down with Baby, holding jittery
bird-bone scapulae to his shoulder. 'Backward

in walking and talking – but so elegant
crawling naked across the floor! A remarkable,

sweet, joyful disposition. Not high spirits, though.'
They know this Baby's different. This is Down's Syndrome

four years before John Langdon Haydon Down
discovers it. 'Strange grimaces. Small for his age.

He shivers when excited. But will lie calm
a long time, on my lap, looking at my face

with a steady, pleased expression, making nice
little bubbling noises when I move his chin.'

VII

A SPOT OF MALARIA IN THE MOLUCCAS

Every day, during the cold and succeeding hot fits, I had nothing to do but think over any subject particularly interesting me.

Alfred Russel Wallace

Using Ternate as a base, Wallace went collecting on the neighbouring island Halmahera. In February 1858 he fell ill there. While ill, he worked out the concept of natural selection, the stage missing from the argument for evolution which Darwin had seen in 1838.

He looks out from the one-room hut
on wooden stilts above a mountain
to the shining ring of the horizon.

A lucid interval, a slime wind between
the liquid shiverings sucking his flesh
like a lamprey. Yes. These are his hands. Yes

his breath again. Down there in Dodinga lagoon
the dory he came in on, like the new moon
at anchorage. Palm silhouettes

wave their black swords against a stretch
of sea like sooty peacocks at a mirror.
Beyond, more islands. Tidore. And Ternate

where he came from: long, indigo crocodilia
nosing Ocean's silver plate. Banana leaves
shit-speckled as if with sweetpea

petals, or with snow, by roosting birds. His heart
is a prayer wheel, spinning. A durian tree
grows out of his ear, sucking his energy.

He feels charred, as if fever were the only thing
beside him in this hut – but that's not true,
there's been the dark, roosting over him

like a panting animal. And a snake too, a question-mark
around his lamp. Reaching for light, he touched
scales and saw a head rear. *Who's disturbing me?*

Too dark, and he too misty, to see detail or identify
the species. He saw it glide out past his beetle specimens –
and the damn pests, eating his specimens – into rain outside.

He feels a blindfold has come off. He sees the claw-track
of the meteor he watched from a dinghy between glass
wave-troughs off Brazil, when his ship the *Helen* burned

Wallace's first collecting expedition, to the Amazon, 1848–52, ended in shipwreck.

and he lost everything and had to start again.
He feels choked, as if the air were a lie. Somewhere
there must be truer oxygen. The fellow who takes care

of him, bringing soup he cannot eat, carries an ironwood spear
and believes, he says, in a better life to come, but no idea
of the devil; nor of hell. He could stay here for ever –

but there's something else to think. How within each species
are tiny variations. *Lorius garrulus*, the red-green
noisy bird. He's seen it everywhere. On islands to the west

there's a patch of yellow on the back. But on Bacan
this mantle-patch is larger, more ornate, of yellow and green
mixed. 'Variations on different islands might become

new species, if circumstances favour.' The heat is huge,
as if he had the sun in bed with him. 'The least fit variation
would perish, the fittest would survive. New species would thus come

into being.' Over two days, on the fever's turning tide,
a smelly rag of a man on a bed of straw and parasites,
he writes, '*On the Tendency of Varieties to Depart*

Indefinitely from the Original Type'. Silence, like a prayer.
Rustle of snakes after rats. Monkeys mating on the roof.
The fever abates. Leaning on the ironwood spear

he walks to the boat as if nothing had happened.
No severing clarity; no black and red before his eyes;
no claim to fancy thinking. Sea, mountain, palm trees –

all the same. They ferry him back to Ternate.
He writes it out, brushing off the green-black powder-mould
that blooms, in this damp heat, on everything organic.

He makes a copy, twenty pages; writes a letter and address. Ternate, March–April 1858.
Down, England. The one man who'll appreciate –
if it's any good, of course – what fever lit in him.

He glances over
at the smoke-blue coast of Halmahera
and gives it to an official for the post.

VIII

A CRUNCH ON THE GRAVEL

Down House,
18 June 1858.

Bright morning. Pinnacle stems of hollyhocks.
Powdery, just-open, lemony flowers. The small white
inner mantle in a blossom of delphinium,
guarding the stamens and pollen, wet with dew and tipped
like a tiny double paintbrush in the same soft china blue.

Wheels of the post-chaise, spinning to a standstill.
A hiss – as of waves dragging over shale. He just happens
to be out here, watching the ants. Sweetsmell
of horse sweat, snort-breath of a cob.
Another package from the Spice Islands.

IX

YOUR WORDS HAVE COME TRUE WITH A VENGEANCE

Letter to the geologist Charles Lyell, 18 June 1858.

'My dear friend, some years ago you recommended me
to read a piece by Wallace. He has today sent the enclosed,
asking me to forward it to you. When I explained my view

to you of Natural Selection, you said to publish soon
or I sh[d] be forestalled. Your words have come true
with a vengeance. If Wallace had my sketch from '42

he could not have made a better abstract.' His big book
is half-written. 'Even his terms now stand as Heads of my
own Chapters. Please return the M.S. He does not say

he wishes me to publish it. But I shall write back at once
of course, and offer to send to any Journal he desires.'
A taste of pepper on his tongue. Through the open door

he sees a wave gather, rear like a cobra, crash over the carpet
towards him. 'So all my originality, whatever it may amount to,
will be smashed. Though my Book, if it have value,

will not be deteriorated. For all the work consists
in application of the theory. I hope you will approve
of Wallace's sketch, that I may tell him what you say.'

X

A WAVE OF SCARLETINA IN THE HOME COUNTIES

Down House,
21 June 1858.

A midsummer epidemic. She trembles for Etty.
For Leonard at school. For them all.

Two years ago she marvelled, with the nation, at the faith
and patience of Dean Tait – who in four weeks lost five

In Lent 1856, Archibald Tait, Dean of Carlisle (later Archbishop of Canterbury), lost five of his six daughters to scarlet fever. In the mid-nineteenth century scarlet fever was one of the leading causes of child mortality and far more malignant than previously, in the seventeenth century, or later, in the twentieth.

of his daughters, ages two to ten, in Scarlet Fever.
Well-wishers sent money for a memorial, a window in Carlisle.

The disease dragon and five girls. 'Going to Eternal Rest.'
She learned his '*Address to God*' by heart. 'You have dealt

mysteriously with us! This Lent You have reclaimed
the jewels You lent: our children. We thank You for

sweet memories of their lives, Your assurance that they went
to the arms of the Good Shepherd, for the one You left –

and for the bright hope You've given
of reunion in heaven, when we shall part no more.'

One child has died in the village. Holding Baby, hour
by hour, she feels the fever soar.

XI

THE COMET

'Etty has a new disease. Dipterithes, or some such name.
A dreadful inflammation in her throat.'
She's fourteen. 'Discharge. A very weak & rapid pulse.'
He's banned from her bedside: his worry's too upsetting.
No chance of comforting her with backgammon.
Will they lose this daughter too? A comet
is crossing the sky. 'Horrific news from India.'

Letter to J. D. Hooker, 23 June 1858.

XII

FORGIVE THIS TRUMPERY LETTER

'I am very sorry to trouble you in so merely personal an affair.
There is nothing in Wallace's sketch which is not
in my own of '44. I could most truly say, & prove,
that I take nothing from him. I sh[d] *now* be glad
to publish my ideas, but cannot persuade myself

Letter to Charles Lyell, Down House, 25 June 1858.

that I can do so honourably.' Edges in his stomach thresh
against each other. 'I would far rather burn
my whole book than that he, or any man, sh[d] think
I behaved in a paltry spirit.' The ground flinches
in the Turkey carpet under his desk.

'I do not believe he originated his views
from anything I wrote to him. We differ only, that I
was led to mine by domestic breeding. I could send
originals to demonstrate I did not steal his doctrine.
I cannot tell if to publish now would not be base.

My good dear friend, this is miserably written.
A trumpery letter, influenced by trumpery feelings.
I fear we may have Scarlet Fever in the House. *C.D.*
Forgive me adding a P.S. – to make the case as strong
as possible against myself. Wallace might say,

"Is it fair to take advantage
of my communicating my ideas, & thus prevent
me forestalling you?" It seems hard to lose
my priority of many years, but I am not sure
that affects the justice of the case. Emma desires

her affectionate thanks, in which I heartily join,
to your wife for her kind note. Etty is very weak
but progressing. The Baby has fever – we hope
not Scarlet but three children in the village are dead
and others at death's door, with terrible suffering.'

XIII

THE TELL-TALE TONGUE

One dreaded symptom of scarlet fever was the 'strawberry tongue'.

Caused – no one knows
yet – by an exotoxin released into the
system by *Streptococcus pyogenes* bacterium.
Starts with a sandpaper rash that blanches upon
pressure and spreads over the whole body, redder in
creases of the elbows, armpits and groin. Pale area around
the lips. Vomiting. Dark fizz of bubbled bile. Hard lumps
in the neck, experts agree, a major feature. White patina
of slimy rime covering the tongue, whose inflamed
papillae grow bigger till the whole thing –
the tongue that is – looks like
a strawberry.

XIV

THE TERRESTRIAL CRUST

Letter to J. D. Hooker, Down House, 29 June 1858.

'Poor Baby died last night. I hope to God he did not suffer
so much as he appeared.' He's writing in the study.
He has just retched: the butler, who holds him in his arms
in violent sickness, carts away the smelly froth.
'He became quite suddenly worse.' A moment on his own.

This week! As if the terrestrial crust had burst
beneath his feet. 'Poor Emma behaved nobly.
It was most blessed relief to see
his poor little innocent face resume
its sweet expression in the sleep of death.

Thank God he will not suffer more
in this world.' His friends propose to read aloud
what Wallace wrote, along with his own work –
like setting two doves free from the Ark
instead of one – to prove each man

has come to Natural Selection alone.
What does it matter? Nature's runes
of agony, cut in a tiny face. 'God bless you.'
He stares at spiders of wet ink. 'You shall hear soon
from me. As soon as I can think.'

XV

THE BLACK AND THE GREEN

Emma upright in black at St Mary's, facing the narrow spire
like a small Dutch wizard's hat. A hover-fly
just above her shoulder on translucent wings.
A little mouth of opened earth by the west door.

Downe Church, 1 July 1858.

Worms will be wriggling away from light.
What is it like, to be disturbed in there?
This mound, beside, is where they laid
baby Mary who reminded Emma of her mother.

He takes Bessy's hand. They all go in. He thinks of words
he's never seen, the ones he asked to be engraved
on Annie's tomb. *A dear good child.* Meanwhile,
this very day, someone is reading other words

On the same day, Wallace's paper written at Ternate and one of Darwin's sketches of his own theory were read out together, in both men's absence, at the Linnaean Society, Burlington House in Piccadilly.

to learned men, giving evolution to the world.
Who'll care? He'll write the book at once.
A mournful one. The infinity of loss. He feels ashamed,
as if his long-fought theories were bad dust

On the Origin of Species.

from someone else's dream. They kneel; they sing.
Redemption after suffering. He looks at Emma's shawl.
'*All Through the Night*': the slow Welsh hymn
he learned with his mother in Chapel, the only tune

anyone's ever heard him try to hum. Flints, mashed
into shape by geothermal pressure: discoloured teeth
in the wall. As they walk out, Bessy pulls to stroke
the grain of an upright in the porch. An oak beam

five hundred years, perhaps, in the making.
Bessy likes things simple, as he does, and true
to their own being. He looks at his children
on bright grass. The little coffin. Black and green.

MY ABOMINABLE VOLUME

I

A PIGEON FANCIER'S MANUAL

Down House, and Isle of Wight, 1858–59.

'This horrid Species thing.' He's got to write it new –
and smaller! Just (just!) summarizing his views.
'My rag of a book. It cost me so much labour
I almost hate it.' They build a billiard room
beside the study. He pots coloured balls like sweets
as a rest from work. She protects him from visitors
and relatives. No one's ill – they take a family holiday
on the Isle of Wight. He finishes in April.
The publisher's reader says, 'Make it a manual

on pigeon-breeding! Forget the rest.
Everyone loves pigeons – it'd be reviewed
by every journal in the land.' John Murray knows
a good thing when he sees one, he'll do a small
edition but it's still too long. Edit. Vomit. Edit.
Shadows in the dawn. Resist the lure
of ever more evidence. He sends it and disappears
for a water cure. 'Severely ill.' In November,
at fifteen shillings, it sells out in one go.

The full title was *On the Origin of Species by Means of Natural Selection, or the Preservation of Favoured Races in the Struggle for Life*. Afterwards, between 1860 and 1872, he took the book through five more editions.

II

THE OPEN WINDOW

There is no greater mystery in the whole world, as it seems to me, than the existence of sexes.

Letter to Henslow, July 1860

In 1860 Darwin started work on his first detailed exposition of the power of natural selection: the fertilization of orchids. He worked on plants for the next decade. It is sexes in plants he is immediately thinking of in 1860.

He's glad that she is glad. He has not publicly
rejected a Creator and he hardly mentioned Man.
'Psychology will now be based on a new foundation:
the acquirement of each necessary power. Capacity
by gradation.' That was all. The soon-to-be
Archbishop of Canterbury explains you can, indeed,
square evolution with a God. 'God operates
through the slow work of natural cause.'

He gets a fan letter from Charles Kingsley, novelist.
'Even better than making the world, God makes
the world make itself.' He watches her smile
at Lenny and open a window for fresh air.
Religion: the burned heart in its thorns. A rock face
shot with quartz on which the sun
shines as it rises, lighting the rock to fire.

III

BIBLICAL

There is a mysterious box come for you, marked Glass but with a kind of gridiron lid as if it had something alive inside.

Emma, Letter to Charles Darwin, 14 December 1862

His supporters sharpen their swords for argument:
he's ill. They debate at Oxford – he
takes a hydropathic cure. Only she knows
what the nights are like. Hysterical weeping,
retching, smells. Days of giddiness. Collapse.

Public reaction to the *Origin* focused on the thing he did *not* mention in it explicitly: human origins. His younger supporters, like Huxley, were glad to take on this argument in public.

'Bessy fails with irregular pulse and her nervous tic.
George has a fever, Lenny frequent bad days
and Etty keeps very weak. A strange inheritance!
My accursed constitution showing itself
in ever a new form.' Don't fathers who feel wrong

1 February 1859.

in themselves locate it in their children? 'Touched
by the sweetness and gentleness
with which he endured, I cannot recall any case
in which pain was so truly poignant.
When the worst attacks come on, he seems almost crushed

The words of a Dr Lane who treated Darwin earlier, in 1857. For a decade after he published the *Origin*, in 1859, Darwin's health was much worse, intermittently, than ever; almost a collapse.

with agony. But they are so stoically born!'
Now it's lunatic farting, vomit, stomach-and-whole-
body ache. These midnight demons, weeping and shakes,
must have organic origin – like everything.
Tears streak the greying stubble on his cheeks.

'I am never comfortable without you.' She cannot leave him,
  day or night, for more than quarter of an hour.
'I hope my life will be short! For to lie
  on the sofa giving nothing but trouble
to the best and kindest of wives, and dear good children,

'Am I a Man and a Brother?' asked a gorilla in a *Punch* cartoon, 18 May 1860, alluding to the Wedgwood medallion and Darwin's own ancestry. After Darwin published *The Descent of Man*, 1871, the ape cartoons increased.

is dreadful.' The pains continue – worse
  when newspapers laugh about apes.
Cartoons, abuse, rude letters; the contempt.
  She writes her own letter. 'I cannot tell
the compassion I have felt

June 1861.

for your suffering these past weeks. Nor my gratitude
  for the cheerful affectionate looks you give
when I know you are miserably uncomfortable.
  My heart has been too full to speak.
I often think of the words, "Thou shalt keep him

in perfect peace whose mind is stayed on Thee."
  I feel presumptuous, writing this to you!
I feel your admirable qualities and feelings.
  I hope you would direct them upwards –
as well as to one who values them

Darwin grew his beard in 1862. It began neat but after long illness in the 1860s it became the straggly prophet-like beard of his old age.

over everything in the world.' He writes back,
  wobbly, faint. On the fold of hers, as long ago.
'God bless you.' Still, they joke. Their humour
  is still whimsical. In a bout of eczema
he grows a beard. He now looks biblical.

THE EXTRA EYE

My father once said to me with a smile that he believed he could write a poem on Drosera, the sundew, on which he was then working.

William Darwin

Privacy grows round him
like fur on a hibernating bear.
For visitors, he sets up a mirror
by the front door on the wall,

angled so he can check them
from the study. 'I care more 1860.
just now for Drosera than the origin
of any species in the world.'

'Nothing in my scientific life
has given me such satisfaction
as the structure of the primula.
The two forms, perfect hermaphrodites,

bear the same relation to each other
as sexes of a mammal.' He publishes a book
on orchids. 'A pleasure to write. 1862.
But whether worth writing I know not

any more than the man in the moon.'
When the sickness is worst
he watches a tendril
spiral clockwise into light.

'The tip of the root
might be compared to the brain.'
Each leaf glows with its own meaning
as if he had a third eye in his forehead

which he could never close.
'Idleness is misery.' The life-forms
tell him their stories, as if he could walk
through the organic world like a door

and touch the source of light.
'We stand in awe before the mystery
of life.' Spores of the giant fern.
The ivory bulb of a crocus.

'My mind has become a machine
for grinding laws
out of large collections of facts.'
He asks a friend in Delhi to recommend

a book on the Indian Mutiny.
They read it together:
she reads to him every afternoon.
1865. He writes a paper on climbing plants

and watches drops of mucilage
glisten on the tentacles of *Drosera*,
the common sundew,
like poison in a fairy tale.

Like the Venus Flytrap, they entice
and then they curl. 'One wing of a gnat
is enough to snap it tight.' She watches him
in the greenhouse, still as a stalking cat,

bent in a caftan of light over stamen,
glands and lanceolate leaf.
Is no distinction safe? 'I know
what he is up to! He's wondering

if Drosera is an animal.' Like a tree
in Kensington Gardens
with a tiger underneath. Like *Flustra*.
Like the polyps in coral reefs.

THE DESCENT OF MAN

I

I THINK I SHALL DISLIKE IT VERY MUCH

He's glad they're out there, young scientists,
giving the world his argument. It's out, it's done –
and he's spent nine years on plants.
Now *The Descent of Man and Selection*
in Relation to Sex. He's got to state, at last,
his vision of 1838, before they married.
'I shall be well abused.' She studies the first draft.

In 1868 he published *The Variation of Animals and Plants under Domestication* and started the book on specifically human origins.

'I think it will be very interesting, but I
shall dislike it very much. It is again putting God
even farther off.' He thinks of an orang-utang
in a pink frock and frills, looking in his eyes,
being generous. Opening his palm
to gift her treasure to him. Many moments in this marriage
have been saved – by both of them – with laughs.

II

MUSCLE AT THE CORNER OF THE MOUTH

The Expression of the Emotions in Man and Animals, published 1872.

'Body and mind are intertwined. A mental image
on its transitory movement through the brain
has a biological response.' He lays it out in sections
like the segments of a worm. 'The links are wonderful

which connect effect with cause.' Anger, painting cells
of the skin with scarlet. 'The mystery of what's between
the body and the mind.' Can the relation of emotional display
to the working of facial muscle be a link between the animal

and human? 'Pallor of fear. Things we do not understand
of our own feelings. The heart – its rate of beating. The rise
and fall of breath. The secretion, in infants only
(Englishmen rarely cry), of tears.'

But Willie, a banker now! Leonard in the Royal Engineers!
Frank a biologist, and working with him! George
an astronomer at Cambridge, discovering the period
of the moon and Earth's internal heat!

'Hurrah for bowels of the Earth and their viscosity, for the Moon
and Heavenly bodies – and for my son George! Oh Lord
what a set of sons I have, all doing wonders!'
Prickly, pale gold Etty – married! Grandchildren!

Letter to George, 1878.

Etty married in 1871. Bessy never married.

But tears in his eyes when he thinks of Annie, still.
He watches an old lady on the train. She's comfortable,
absorbed. 'Suddenly the *anguli oris depressores*,
muscles that pull down corners of the mouth, contract.'

Expression of the Emotions, Chapter 7.

He sees a tear; the lips ridge in; a shift of subcutaneous fat.
He knows what's going on. That spasm of negative smile –
'Like shadow on the face of loss. Some painful recollection
was going through her mind, like that of a long-lost child.'

III

THEY GIVE HIM A COAT OF FUR

January 1880. This year Darwin published *The Power of Movement in Plants*.

A surprise – to keep out cold. A soft mountain,
colour of Alaskan forest in the dusk, each hair
a dark blaze of loam. He'd never buy it for himself!
It's a conspiracy: Frank leaves it on the table
in the study, furry side outward, at three,
with a letter from all the children. He'll find it
when he goes for his walk at four. They tell
their mother just before. 'So she can see the fun!'

He stands stock-still. Then puts it on behind the screen
that hides his vomiting. One arm. Two. It hangs heavy,
nearly to the floor. He feels like a dream of the north –
of hibernation – of the Earth's internal heat. He comes out
to the hall, shrouded in animal, a priest
with tears in his eyes. 'Wonderful comfort! Last time I went
to London, I did not get over the cold for several days.
I think it does very well being loose and long.'

But he would not be himself – they tease him –
if he did not protest! So worried, always,
about money. Every Accounts Day he would say,
'Bread and cheese only from now on!'
Frank remembers being young enough to believe him.
'You have been shamefully extravagant
to spend so much on your old father –
however deeply you may have pleased him.'

HE DISCOVERS A PORTRAIT OF HIS MOTHER

He watches brass handles on his brother's coffin
    disappear in earth. Edinburgh. A riding tour in Wales.
Experiments in the toolshed. And now the west door

of Downe Church. He observes the shine
    on blades of grass like emerald wire.
It grows sparse like that under the yews.

'I have neither strength nor heart
    to begin an investigation lasting years,
the only thing I enjoy. I must look forward

to Downe graveyard as the sweetest place on earth!'
    But in a box from London, from a brother
who never married, he turns up an oval frame –

a miniature – a pretty face kept secret
    all these years. He's an expert, now, on faces;
on muscle-shadow round the mouth.

'I wrote to my elder sister Caroline
    because I had no recollection. She said
it was a good likeness, this sweet, this kind expression.'

In 1881 Darwin published his last contribution to science, *The Formation of Vegetable Mould through the Action of Worms*. In August, Erasmus died and his effects were sent to Down.

I MADE HIS COFFIN JUST THE WAY HE WANTED IT, ALL ROUGH

Darwin died on 19 April 1882.

They'll bury him beside his brother. The village carpenter –
who made his instruments, and boxes 'for his queer
experiments' – knows what he likes. Simple and plain.
An old friend will take the service. The publican
at the George and Dragon prepares for crowds.

But you're forgetting London. The Royal Society. The Dean
of Westminster. A notorious freethinker, in the Abbey?
Questions in Parliament. An *Evening Standard* campaign:
'A man who brought such honour to the English name
should not lie in an obscure grave.'

'It gave us a pang not to have him rest quietly here.
But we knew his gracious and grateful nature
would have wished to accept the acknowledgement.'
The carpenter complains. 'I made it as he wanted it, no polish,
nothing, just as it left the bench. His coffin was not wanted!

Down House, 26 April 1882.

The one they sent, you could see your face in it.'
Black horses. The difficult, blue-glossy manes. The bearing rein.
The hearse with her spray of white lilies. She watches him depart
on those sixteen miles to London. She always prayed
they'd never part. She looked after him, moment by moment. Now

there's one more thing. Surely the God of Love will not cast out
a good man who searched, so earnestly, for truth. Memories.
Ageing. Their youth. *It is almost worth being sick*
to be nursed by you. 'Oh that I could remember more!
But it was the same loving gratitude, many times a day.'

*

Let's leave her in the drawing-room, at the piano. 'His tenderness
    seemed to increase. The last twelve years were happiest of all,
most overflowing with affection.' She's looking at rain. At April grass.
    'She lived through her desolation,' the children will say, 'alone.'
This garden they made together. Its life beyond the glass.

A NOTE ABOUT THE AUTHOR

Ruth Padel is a prizewinning poet, a Fellow of the Royal Society of Literature and of the Zoological Society of London, and the first writer in residence at Somerset House, London. Her poetry collections include *Rembrandt Would Have Loved You*, *Voodoo Shop* and *The Soho Leopard*, all short-listed for the T. S. Eliot Prize. She has also published two much-loved books on reading contemporary poetry, *52 Ways of Looking at a Poem* and *The Poem and the Journey*, and an acclaimed nature book, *Tigers in Red Weather*, which was short-listed for the Kiriyama Prize.